DATE DUE

MAR 2 6 1993			
JUL 0 6 1993			
AUG 1 1 1994			

An Illustrated Handbook to

SURVIVING
Family Camp Outs

By Edward G. Dorn II
The Father Of 16 Active Children

CEL Publications
Palatine, Illinois

An Illustrated Handbook To Surviving Family Camp Outs

Printed in the United States of America. All inquiries should be addressed to:
      CEL Publications,
      PO Box 553
      Palatine, IL 60078-0553.

Library of Congress Cataloging-in-Publication Data:
Dorn, Edward G.
An Illustrated Handbook To Surviving Family Camp Outs
by Edward G. Dorn II.
p. cm.
Includes index.
1. Camping. 2. Family recreation.
I. Title.
GV191.7.D67 1992
796.54–dc20   92-5007 CIP

ISBN 0-9631806-0-6

Printed in the United States of America

Although the author and publisher have exhaustively researched all sources to ensure the accuracy and completeness of the information contained in this book, we assume no responsibility for errors, inaccuracies, omissions or any inconsistency herein. The source for much of this survival information is the Department of Army *Special Forces Field Guide*.

Cover Photo: An Autumn camp out for the Dorn family in their favorite place — Door County, Wisconsin.

The Handbook: How it All Came About

Keeping track of four attractive daughters, twelve competitive sons, three superactive grandchildren, two playful dogs and a traveling cat can be a survival challenge — both indoors and outdoors. The logistics of moving about requires mammoth preparation and extra patience.

When we travel our family on the road resembles a convoy made up of cars, trucks and RVs. We always manage — and overcome — a few vehicle breakdowns and flat tires. Eventually we arrive and set up camp for inspired family outdoor recreation and activities. The most important area is the 24-hour-a-day kitchen managed by my wife, Ceil. This area never seems to shut down. There are always plenty of assistant cooks and KPs to help. Our family believes the key to any successful camp out is good eating. Most of Ceil's outdoor recipes are in this book and in her new cookbook *An Illustrated RV & Over the Coals Cookbook*.

We also decided to include the essential camp out basics, what we learned in the last twenty years of camping, most of our family experiences outdoors and how we survived them all together. They are all in this book. Hope you enjoy the experience of traveling along.

DEDICATION
To my mother and father, who taught us
how to love the outdoors.

ACKNOWLEDGMENTS
The inspiration given by my wife, Cecilia,
and our sixteen children.
My fellow campers who are responsible for
much of this information.

CREDITS
Photography ....Steve Dorn and Kathleen Dorn
Graphic Design ....Gregg Woods
Typesetting..Linda Dorn and Elayne Sivertsen
Editing by..Al Davis

Table of Contents

PART I

How to Start and Plan a Family Outdoor Camping Trip

To begin, you must decide where and how long. This includes the time required to get there, enjoy yourself and travel back safely.

Your resources are an important consideration. This should include, besides financial funds, a measure of your inner strength and long-term durability. When all this is added up, you are now ready for inspiration, even suggestions from friends, and others who are experienced campers.

By the way, it's always a good idea to tag along with these friends if they are willing to break you in. Otherwise, we recommend an overnighter to start. In the meantime, start gathering information. U.S. government agencies and state travel offices are a valuable source of information regarding our national park system. We have a complete listing of these agencies in the back of the book for your convenience.

You should check on the permits required in national parks and forests. A campground directory of both private and public campgrounds is available from Woodall Publishing in Bannockburn, IL. Detailed maps of how to get there are illustrated in this over 600-page directory. All private parks listed are quality inspected and rated by Woodall. RV service and accessory locations and park attractions are also listed.

The National Park System

National park system color map folds out to 16½ by 23½ inches

Planning ahead will make your trip more rewarding. Here are some suggestions.

Openings and closings vary from park to park. So do visiting hours. It's best to write to the park for specific details regarding hours, parking, facilities and transportation services available to and within the boundaries of the park.

Start with the visitor center when arriving. Literature, exhibits, slides and sometimes even movies are part of the park orientation.

If you do not like crowds, consider camping in the spring or fall. There are some 170 national parklands and historic sites to choose from that are relatively new or located away from main highways. Send for the *Lesser-Known Areas* booklet available from the Superintendent of Documents, U.S. Government Printing Office, Washington, D.C., 20402 (ask for

stock number 024-055-00911-6).

For entrance fee savings, you may want to check out the Golden Eagle Passport available at national park entrances (good for one year). Senior citizens, 62 or older, are eligible for a free lifetime Golden Age Passport that covers admissions and provides a 50 percent discount on campground and other user fees. There are also discounts for the disabled.

Some parks ration backcountry use to protect fragile land and water resources. You must apply for a permit (it's free) from the park rangers. Some require reservations. Campsites may be used for recreational vehicles, tents, or both. Most are available on a first-come, first-serve basis. Camping fees vary. For groups, reservations may be required. State and federal regulations may apply to fishing and hunting.

For additional information and assistance regarding National Parks, contact the Office of Public Inquiries (202) 208-4747.

A full size 16½" x 23½" color map of the national park system is available from the Consumer Information Center, Pueblo, CO 61009.

The Next Step – Rough Out Your Trip

Plan your movements with the maps available. If you are a member of the AAA (Automobile Association of America), you can obtain road maps with your trip detailed. Maps can also be obtained for the United States from the U.S. Geological Survey (see the outdoor reference section).

9

Van/station wagon air mattress

The Most Economical Start

What you are now driving can be modified with a roof rack. A cargo box can be attached even if your vehicle is only a sedan. Cargo boxes vary in design, but they can add 20 cubic feet to your vehicle's capacity. They should be of an aerodynamic design, watertight, lockable and made of fiberglass. These boxes are easy to install. Quality boxes can be purchased for under $400.

What You Need to Live in the Wilderness

If you prepare for both warm and cold weather, you will need over a hundred items. For survival, you must think of the basics such as clothing, food, personal comfort, transportation, sleeping, maintenance and emergency. Your needs will vary from trip to trip. We suggest you prepare a list using our checklist as a guide. Most of the gear can be obtained in any discount store. You may want to visit a camping store for some of the specialty items. Some camping stores will rent outdoor equipment — a good way to start. Keep in mind, however, that you will forget something. The best list is always developed from experience and includes, of course, good companions (and helpers). This is a *must* on any list of needs in the wilderness.

Sleeping Gear

The sleeping bag may be the most important of all general camp out gear. Without rest and comfort, your stay will be short. Your bag should assure a warm sleep at 20 degrees minimum. If you camp in the winter, you'll need more insulation. The larger the bag, the better. Some sleepers shift and toss at night. A slide fastener that runs clear around the bottom is a good idea. There are all types of sleeping bags available. Backpackers

'Mummy style' bags

will require lighter types. Some are designed to zip together in pairs. Visit your camping store for ideas. The peer of all portable outdoor mattresses is a tough air mattress. My first experience with one was bivouacking in the army. I slept like a log. You must make sure no sharp objects are underneath your air mattress. And always carry a patch kit and small pump just in case. If you are afraid of a possible leak, then the next choice is a foam pad that will roll up. Cots and hammocks are other choices, and they are better in warm weather.

Flexible Clothing

The best defense against temperatures that vary from 85 degrees at noon and then drop to subfreezing at night is layers of clothing. I'm remembering some Minnesota experiences in July that taught us this flexible system that allows you to add or remove layers: 1. Underwear. 2. Regular Clothing. 3. Insulation. 4. Outer Garments. This way you are prepared for heat, rain or cold. It's also more comfortable at night.

The Family Getaway Weekend

In today's world, where long vacations are becoming the exception, RVs fit the two-day, three-day or extended getaway. The kids have to attend school or go to work during the week. Keep in mind the traveling advantages a RV offers. You can store camping gear and equipment on board and be ready to go on a minute's notice. Just fill the fresh water tank and gas up. Use our Family Camp Out Check List as a reminder and you're on your way to an instant family gathering in the outdoors.

Our "Idea Jogging" Family Camp Out Checklist

(Expand on it!)

Shelter Gear

- ☐ Tent
- ☐ Field pack
- ☐ Carry-all bag
- ☐ Shelter items
- ☐ Nylon net/screens
- ☐ Ground liner
- ☐ Strong rope/pegs

Sleeping Gear

- ☐ Sleeping bags
- ☐ Air mattresses
- ☐ Inflatable pillow
- ☐ Blankets

Accessories

- ☐ Compass
- ☐ Flashlight
- ☐ Extra batteries
- ☐ Multifunction pocket knife
- ☐ Hammer hatchet
- ☐ Set of tools
- ☐ Folding saw
- ☐ Canteen
- ☐ Cup/mess kit
- ☐ Filleting knife & board
- ☐ Thermos
- ☐ Tire pump

Cooking Gear

- ☐ Utensils — pots and pans
  (See our cooking utensil team — Part III)
- ☐ Gelatin molds
- ☐ Cutting board
- ☐ Can opener
- ☐ Disposable coolers
- ☐ Aluminum foil *(lots)*

- ☐ Covered grill
- ☐ Charcoal/tinder material
- ☐ LP stove/oven attachment
- ☐ Propane gas
- ☐ Stove sparker
- ☐ Wood matches
- ☐ Low-power appliances (12V)

Food/Supplies

- ☐ Fresh water
- ☐ Juices/soda
- ☐ Dried foods
- ☐ Canned foods
- ☐ Cereals
- ☐ Snacks/vitamins
- ☐ Condiments/spices
- ☐ Paper plates/cups
- ☐ Detergent/ disinfectant
- ☐ Garbage bags *(lots)*
- ☐ Soap/toothpaste
- ☐ Toilet tissue/paper towels

Outdoor Clothing

Warm Weather

- ☐ Underwear *(lots)*
- ☐ Extra cotton socks
- ☐ Cotton clothes
- ☐ Short sleeve shirts
- ☐ Shorts/bathing suit
- ☐ Lightweight jacket

Cold Weather

- ☐ Insulated suit/hooded
- ☐ Heavy gloves/ ski mask
- ☐ Wool socks/ sweaters/scarves

- ☐ Heavy long-sleeve shirts & pants
- ☐ Long john underwear

All Weather

- ☐ Good boots *(water repellent)*
- ☐ Rain gear/hooded
- ☐ Extra clothes *(to change into when wet)*
- ☐ Comfortable hat or cap
- ☐ Work gloves

Safety

- ☐ Life preservers
- ☐ Life jackets
- ☐ All-purpose fire extinguisher
- ☐ Bike helmet/gloves

Hygiene/Health/ First Aid

- ☐ Vitamins
- ☐ Medication *(if applicable)*
- ☐ Mouth wash/ antiseptic
- ☐ Insect & tick repellent
- ☐ Buffered aspirin
- ☐ Anti-acid tablets
- ☐ Salt & chlorine tablets
- ☐ Hot water bottle
- ☐ First aid kit *(See First Aid & Medical Emergency Kit Checklist on page 86)*

Personals

- ☐ Toothbrush
- ☐ Flossing kit
- ☐ Wash cloth/towels
- ☐ Sun tan lotion/ sun screen

- ☐ Sun glasses
- ☐ Mirror/comb
- ☐ Shaving gear
- ☐ Shoe polish
- ☐ Nail clippers
- ☐ Body deodorant

Activities

- ☐ Binoculars
- ☐ Fishing gear
- ☐ Snare wires
- ☐ AM/FM radio
- ☐ Camera
- ☐ Game boards *(Magnetic)*
- ☐ Sketch pad
- ☐ Books/magazines
- ☐ Paper, pencil & pen

Transportation

- ☐ Maps/directories
- ☐ Cross-country skis *(Winter)*
- ☐ Canoe/paddles
- ☐ Trail bikes
- ☐ Inflatable craft/ outboard motor

Miscellaneous

- ☐ Rags/polish
- ☐ Brooms/mops
- ☐ Plastic pails
- ☐ Duct tape
- ☐ _____
- ☐ _____
- ☐ _____
- ☐ _____
- ☐ _____
- ☐ _____
- ☐ _____
- ☐ _____

PART II

Some RV and Boat Choices

Author getting fishing tips from son, James

RVs – A Fast Growing Industry

One out of ten American families own a recreation vehicle. And one in twenty families will rent one this year. For the camper age fifty and over, the class A is the leading choice. Another reason for the growing popularity of motor homes is the possibility of their qualifying as a second home, giving the owner the tax benefits of a second home mortgage.

Consider Renting

This may be the best way to start, but keep in mind that some dealers have a waiting list in the summer.

Visit a recreational vehicle dealer and check out luxurious class As, minihomes, fifth wheelers, slide-out rooms, travel trailers, basement truck campers and sporty camping trailers. Be sure to test drive to find out which type handles best with you on the road. If your goal is outdoor comfort, you'll want a model offering a refrigerator (including small freezer), a multiburner stove, a stainless steel sink with running water, two fold-out tables, a sleeping compartment, a toilet facility and a place to take a quick shower. Plus plenty of storage space and extra water storage.

Another advantage of RVs in the wilderness is protection against the elements and animals. A rainy day or evening becomes just raindrops beating on your metal roof. Your camp set up and break down is less time consuming too.

What about Four-Wheel Drive?

The biggest attraction of a four-wheel-drive vehicle is not getting stuck. Wherever you are camping, a 4 x 4 truck opens nature's doors a little wider. You can negotiate old logging trails with

fiberglass exterior skin model with an automatic lifting system. These aerodynamic tow trailers compare to the most expensive motor homes in comfort and facility.

ease in any season. The most remote areas can be reached for camping, canoeing, fishing, etc. Just add a roof rack or a bike carrier and new trails are ready to blaze.

Other factors to weigh are the additional cost and the fact that two-wheel drive is sufficient for most roads. However, it's a great feeling in the outdoors to know you have this extra performance when challenged by mother nature.

Haul a Fold-Down Camper

Any rear-wheel drive vehicle should be able to handle a low-profile camper featuring a roof lifter system. Just crank it up and down. Be sure there's proper water runoff and that the duck canvas is double-stitched for heavy use. It's very economical to use. A self-draining ice box and portable stove are all you need. You may also want to consider a

Cottages on Wheels

Invest in a people hauler/tow vehicle and travel trailer (fifth wheeler type) if you enjoy room and comfort. Look for aerodynamic styling for more stable towing. With all the options available, you can just about design your own floor plan. This vehicle is ideal for just dropping on your lot year-round.

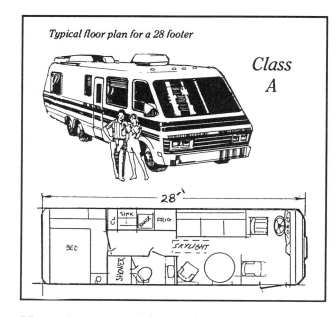

Typical floor plan for a 28 footer

Class
A

The fastest growing type of RVs is the class B motor home, which is basically a camper van. These vans can be utilized in many ways. As the illustrated floor plan shows, they have plenty of room during the day and an area in which to dine, and at night a choice of twin beds or a roomy double.

Take a Tour of a Class C Motor Home

To better demonstrate the progress and comfort level of a modern motor home we invite you to tour our choice of RV traveling — a type C motor vehicle, specifically one in the 26-foot range. The main difference between an A-type motor home and a C-type is the cut-away design. The RV manufacturer builds the living area on an automotive

chassis that includes the cab. The rear section of the cab is cut-away — allowing movement from the cab into the living area. The floor is raised to add "basement storage" space.

Motor Homes — Three Classes

Let's start with the class A motor home. These RVs fully equipped may run close to $100,000 new. For this price tag, expect a lounge, sofa bed, swivel chairs, TV and VCR, galley with water filter and purifier, enclosed bath and rear master bedroom, quality woodwork, expensive upholstery and rich carpeting. On the outside, plan on having an attached screened tent for summer. This type of RV can be lived in year-round as you explore the country.

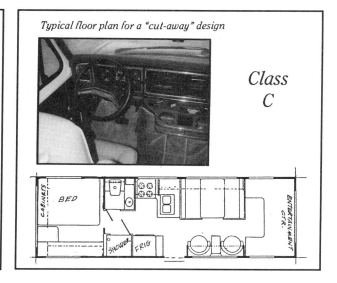

Typical floor plan for a camper van

Class
B

Typical floor plan for a "cut-away" design

Class
C

Let's start our tour at the entry and check out the galley first. You'll find warm water from an electronic ignition water heater, a four-burner range with an oven, and an overhead microwave oven. The galley offers loads of storage space above and below, plus a large refrigerator/freezer, and even has a pantry.

Next, let's visit the travelers' rest area.

Pictured Above: Storage cabinets. Below: The galley. Inset: Overhead microwave oven.

15

Top: Large refrigerator and freezer. Lower left: The pantry. Lower center: Double bed, overhead cabinets and nightstand.
Lower right: Showers "on the go." Upper right: Recreational area.

The roomy passageway leads to a bed, overhead cabinets and a nightstand. Continuing, we find a walk-through bath for showers "on the go." Now, on to the dining and recreational section — an area of comfort with plush stain-free carpeting and wood finishes. Swivel chairs round out the entertainment center, which features an AM/FM cassette stereo with four speakers, color TV and VCR.

16

Our model enjoys a 460-cubic-inch engine that powers all the comforts of home on the road. Other features include a 42-gallon waste water tank, a 25-gallon water system, a 6-gallon water heater, a 70-pound LP gas capacity, a furnace (24 x 1,000 BTU), two deep-cycled batteries for back-up power, generator and towing hitch. And we are still discovering features from the manufacturer. They must have forgotten something, but we doubt it.

Extra beds, designed to sleep six, come about with bunks stored above the cab and under the dinette table. There's plenty of built-in storage space, closet space and privacy in this well-lit motor home.

Let's move to the outside through a clear window entry door with a power step. An exterior entertainment table can be pulled out, and there's plenty of basement storage space for a maneuverable RV boat and hook-ups for power, water and a sewer system.

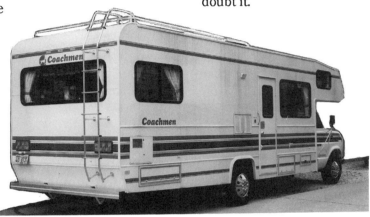

Dump valves for waste holding tanks(42-gallons). Includes faucet.

12-volt demand water pump with hook-ups for fresh water. Also storage for hoses.

Propane tank—70-pound LP gas capacity.

Water heater—fast recovery, 6-gallon capacity.

Cooling unit for refrigerator/ freezer—ammonia or generator driven (with outlet).

Generator—4000 Watt power source. For inside and outside hook-ups.

Storage compartment.

Maneuverable boat compartment.

Illustrated Guide to RVs

Vehicle Types	Design	Size/Description	Approximate Cost Average
Motor Home Class A		20 feet – 35 feet long. Aerodynamically built from the chassis up. Unit constructed on bare motor vehicle rail chassis.	$60,000. Fully equipped, can run as high as $100,000.
Motor Home Class B		Camper vans with sleeping, kitchen and toilet facilities. Various hook-ups. Top extension for added head room.	$30,000
Motor Home Class C *Compact*		Compact — less than 6,500 pounds. Built on an automotive-manufactured cab and chassis.	Varies
Low profile		Chopped van over 6,500 pounds. Under eight feet high. Built on an automotive-manufactured van frame with attached cab section.	$35,000
Mini		26 feet – 28 feet long. Over eight feet high. Built on an automotive-manufactured van frame with attached cab section.	Under $50,000
Campers Truck		Slides into pickup truck. Access can be removed and stored on supports.	$8,000 (doesn't include truck)
Towables *Travel trailer*		15 feet – 35 feet long. Three kinds: box type, aerodynamic type (aluminum) and telescoping hard side design.	$13,000 (range from $7,000 – 75,000)
Fifth wheel		18 feet – 35 feet long. Requires truck fifth wheel. Hitch goes in the cargo bed of the truck. Towing ease. Diverse floor plans possible.	$20,000
Fold-Down Camper Trailer		Most have hard tops — some fold into a complete tent. Just crank up and down. Economical to use.	$4,000
Conversions *Van*		Modified van for adding sofa beds, swivel chairs, cabinets and tables. Special conversions for the handicapped.	$22,000 (Up to $50,000 for new van conversion)
Bus		Diesel-powered rear engine vehicles with refurbished interiors. Complete capability.	$200,000 to $450,000

For RV Accessories and Related Products

We recommend you look into Camping World, a retail chain of camping equipment stores with  supercenters across the country. It also offers free camping catalogs featuring RV antennas, air conditioners, refrigerators, generators, AC/DC remote controlled TV's, etc. Just about everything from an insulated vent cover to an RV satellite system. There's a Presidents Club at Camping World you can join that saves 10 percent on products, parts and service. Call 1-800-626-5944 for additional information.

Maneuverable Boat for RV's

This water-ready two-piece fiberglass foam injected hull provides positive flotation for two adults (without tube). This portable and stable craft can be used as a shallow draft fishing platform, bay cruiser, or bumper boat to a duck blind. Weighing 110 pounds (hull with tube), it's a perfect mate to an RV vehicle.

Outboard motor: Gasoline to 5 horsepower or electrical troller to 36 pounds thrust. Options available. Glass bottom and heavy duty canvas. Call Water Venture at 1-800-356-9479 for additional information.

Boat Selections

After selecting your RV, the next big choice for the fisher is a boat. Modern boats are made from aluminum, fiberglass, steel or wood. The most popular for fresh water are aluminum or fiberglass because they usually require less maintenance. Fiberglass is easier to repair if damage occurs.

Selecting a hull design depends on how and where the boat will be used. Most powerboats feature a planing hull type. For big water, a displacement hull is ideal for moving smoothly. A variety of multihull designs are available, starting with cathedral and twin hull developments. The power source for small boats (under 20 feet) is an outboard two-cycle (or inboard/outboard) engine. There are also V-8 outboards that can provide up to 300 horsepower. The size of the motor for a boat should be based on load and power capacities. You want a properly powered boat that provides safety, speed and economy even in the roughest winds and waters. Today's trend is to match up the boat and motor as a package deal. Visit marinas, the boatyards and local shops and ask plenty of questions. For additional input, ask friends who are boat owners. Also check out the latest styles in skipper caps.

Boat Requirement Checklist	
☐	Size of length at water line and transom width
☐	Hull design
☐	Materials (hull)
☐	Power source
☐	Horsepower capacity

PART III

Creative Eating Outdoors

I t's very important how you pack food for traveling. You'll save egg breakage by storing them in protective plastic containers. Plastic Ziploc bags and clean plastic containers are the perfect way to keep foods separated while they are stored in the cooler. Sterilize old plastic jugs and use them for lemonade, fruit juices and fresh water. Organized packing will make meal preparation on the road much easier.

Picnics can be set up in minutes when plastic containers turn into serving dishes and a variety of drinks are poured from

Plastic containers

handy plastic containers. A tip for coolers: freeze quarts of milk, tea, coffee and drinking water before you leave home. This will keep the other contents even colder in the cooler.

Cooking Inside and Outside (or Both)

A well-equipped camper makes this job almost like home cooking. Highway rest stops with a cooler and two burner stove fulfilling most of your needs become energy restoration picnics. Your outside cooking set up can be as simple as a little charcoal hibachi and a station wagon tailgate for a table. Propane

Charcoal hibachi

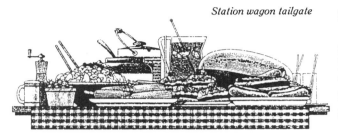

Station wagon tailgate

stoves can also be easily set up (some units can be adjusted for use as heaters on chilly days). For those who wish to travel light — backpackers, etc. — a compact (no bigger than a soup can) single-burner butane stove is the answer. One design features a detachable handled cover that doubles as a cup or pot. See your camping store for these lightweight space savers. A quick checklist for cooking utensils is provided below.

Our Cooking Utensil Team Checklist

- ☐ Cast iron skillet with cover — 10-inch
- ☐ Teflon™ — omelet pan — 10-inch
- ☐ Teflon™ — aluminum pan – 8½-inch
- ☐ Six-quart kettle with top
- ☐ Pots — a variety of quart sizes
- ☐ Pie tins/pizza pans
- ☐ An aluminum and no-scratch spatula
- ☐ Cutting knife, holding fork and spoon scoop
- ☐ Bottled gas stove (pressurized cartridge)
- ☐ Small outdoor grill (legs removed and packed in plastic bag), charcoal, lighter fluid and wooden matches
- ☐ Egg beater and corkscrew
- ☐ Swiss army knife
- ☐ Eating utensils, measuring cup

Selecting a Camp Stove

We like our outdoor covered cooker, as you'll see in the outdoor recipes section. However, a two-burner stove has its place too, especially when the weather is cold. You can choose from several types; each has its advantages and disadvantages.

Two-burner propane stove

Let's start with unleaded gasoline. This type is easily the cheapest and also the most volatile when compared to kerosene or white gas as a fuel. Petroleum-fueled stoves require adequate ventilation at all times. Our choice is a refillable LP type stove with multiburners, and an attachable fold-down oven for baking. It always puts out good heat and is just easier to use. It is heavier — so backpackers may want to look further. Butane stoves are light and require only seconds to replace the cartridge. They don't run as hot as the other types but are fine for warming food. Sterno™ canned heat is another way to warm food and coffee that requires little room. Keep a couple of cans on hand, especially for serving trays outside.

Camp oven

What's on the Menu?

Our military forces eat well in the field. The main reason is organized dietary planning and, of course, the right cooking equipment for serving warm and nourishing food. The day of missing a square meal should not include camp outs. We suggest you plan a rough menu for each day on the road, campground or trail. Draw up your shopping list. Consider cereals, instant cocoa and coffee, powdered juice mixes, canned tuna, salmon and canned meats. Also instant potatoes, soups and puddings. If you must travel light, include freeze-dried foods, they maintain more than 90

21

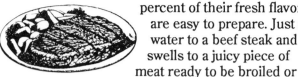

percent of their fresh flavor and are easy to prepare. Just add water to a beef steak and it swells to a juicy piece of meat ready to be broiled or pan fried. A sizzling freeze-dried beef or chicken in sauce is a break from burgers and saves time (and storage space). It's no problem to prepare a mouth-watering meal such as swiss steak with gravy, whipped potatoes and peas, serving two or four.

Try Something New

Special cookbooks for campers are available from Woodall Publishing Co. and CEL Publications, which publishes the book by my wife, Ceil — An Illustrated *RV & Over the Coals Cookbook* (see the outdoor reference section on page 97).

In the meantime, we suggest you try some of our tested recipes in the next part of this book. There's something there for everyone and remember, a camping trip is a vacation. Ask around for what your fellow campers would like to eat. Try to please everyone, no matter how bizarre the menu becomes. Have fun, try some new ideas and ways. Ethnic cooking and eating is a wonderful experience. Starting with only a can or box is a creative cooking challenge that can be very rewarding.

Camp Out Cooking Equivalent Measures and Temperatures

Fluid Measures

3 teaspoons	1 tablespoon
2 tablespoons	1 fluid ounce
8 fluid ounces	1 cup
2 cups	1 pint
2 pints	1 quart
4 quarts	1 gallon

Other Measures

1,000 milligrams	1 gram
28 grams	1 ounce
16 ounces	1 pound

Cooking Temperatures

Slow, slow	250 – 275°F
Slow	300 – 325°F
Moderate	350 – 375°F
Hot	400 – 425°F
Hot, hot	450 – 475°F
Broil	500 – 525°F

Oven Temperatures

°F	°C	°F	°C
200	93	375	191
225	107	400	204
250	121	425	218
275	135	450	232
300	149	475	246
325	163	500	260
350	177	525	274

Defrost Guide

	In refrigerator	Room temperature
Frozen meat, large	5 – 8 hours per pound	3 – 4 hours per pound
Frozen meat, small	2¹/₂ – 4 hours per pound	1¹/₂ – 2 hours per pound

Altitude Temperatures for Boiling Water

°F	°C	Altitude
212	100	Sea level
208	98	2,000 feet
203	95	5,000 feet
194	90	10,000 feet
185	85	15,000 feet

PART IV

Outdoor Recipes

Family Style

The best part of any meal is the gathering of family and friends.
Good food is always enhanced by fellowship and harmony at the table.

Breakfast

Brian's Brunch

Our son Brian is a chef who also enjoys cooking outdoors. His work of art is an array of selections simmering on an outdoor cooker, a wood fire and several sterno cans. It starts with opened cans (lids still attached) of:

Corned beef hash
Meatballs in sauce
Roast beef hash

These cans rest on rocks and are warmed around the low wood fire (occasionally turned with gloved hands). Fried eggs or custom omelettes (as you like them, including egg substitute) are prepared on greased aluminum foil over a pyramid-style charcoal fire. Bacon, smoked sausage and sliced ham are set on foil around Brian's egg center. Bread and English muffins wrapped in foil become toasted when placed around the wood fire.

Create your omelette with...
3 eggs beaten or
3/4 cup egg substitute

Other options
1 slice cheddar cheese
1 slice American cheese
1 slice brick cheese
White onions, chopped
Green pepper, chopped
Mushrooms, drained-sliced
Black olives, drained-sliced
Dash salt and pepper
Margarine for cooking

These ingredients are mixed, cooked on both sides and slid on your plate with extra ham, bacon and smoked sausage surrounding the omelette. Warmed English muffins are the base for the meatballs in sauce. Also served on the side (out of warm cans) are the two kinds of hashes.

Canned fruit cocktail is the dessert choice mixed in with some fresh berries or cherries. Somehow it all comes together and everyone eats more than they should. Every trip features a Brian Breakfast Brunch and a long walk afterwards.

Egg Substitutes (or whites only)

The only way to enjoy eggs and reduce your daily intake of cholesterol is by using only the whites of eggs. You'll never miss the yolks with this combination of taste.

3/4 cup of egg substitutes or whites
only (equals 3 eggs)
1 green pepper, chopped
1 small yellow onion, chopped
1 small can mushrooms, drained
1 small can tomato sauce
2 tablespoons olive oil
Dash salt and pepper

'Veggi' Omelette (no cholesterol)

How to make a perfect omelette everytime.

Beat eggs. In a 10-inch omelette pan, saute peppers and onions slowly in olive oil. When half-cooked, add tomatoes, garlic, salt and pepper. Simmer until soft. Add eggs and raise fire. Cover for one minute. Take off cover, lift edges of eggs. Tip pan slightly to allow liquid egg run off from edges. Re-cover and cook another two minutes. Fold omelette over and count to ten. Slide omelette out of pan.

Suggested healthful mates are smoked turkey sausage or turkey ham slices. Also, oat bran toast.

Breakfast

Other Ideas for Avoiding Cholesterol

· ·

Instant oatmeal (with fruit)
Bran flakes (with fruit)

Just add hot water to your instant oatmeal or skim milk to your bran flakes and you have a cholesterol-fighting breakfast ready in minutes. Don't forget fresh fruit, too — it's a great way to limit eggs. (There are approximately 274 milligrams of cholesterol per egg and the daily dietary guideline for both women and men is under that amount).

Banana French Toast

· ·

4 eggs
1/4 cup 2% milk
1 teaspoon vanilla
1 cup mashed ripe bananas (blend with
    beater or blender until smooth)
10 to 12 slices whole wheat or oat bran
    bread
1 teaspoon sugar
Dash nutmeg or cinnamon and salt
Touch of cooking spray

Beat eggs, add other ingredients (except bread) and pour in shallow dish. Dip slices on both sides. Cook in hot sprayed skillet until golden brown (both sides). Serves five.

Cherry/Blueberry Pancakes

· ·

Makes 20 whole wheat pancakes with fruit inside.

1/2 cup blueberries
1/2 cup cherries, diced
1/2 cup whole wheat flour
2 beaten eggs
2 teaspoons baking powder
2 cups 2% milk
1/2 cup flour
1 tablespoon brown sugar
1 tablespoon vegetable oil
    or melted butter
Dash salt

Combine the flours and baking powder in a large bowl. In another bowl, place the eggs, milk and oil or butter. Stir in the dry ingredients. For each pancake, pour approximately 1/4 cup of mixture on a lightly oiled grill or frying pan. Sprinkle each pancake with a mixture of cherries and blueberries. Watch for bursting bubbles and then flip over. Make sure the bottom is well browned. Repeat on other side. Serve hot with any of fruit sauces and toppings recommended.

25

Breakfast

Apple Honey

Mouth-watering sweetness with a tang for toast and pancakes, — dessert, too.

3 tart peeled apples, chopped
1 cup apple cider
3 teaspoons margarine
Dash ground cinnamon

Beat or blend all ingredients until smooth. Warm in a small sauce pan before serving.

Fresh Fruit Mix

Blend the following ingredients, spoon over pancakes or french toast.

1 cup strawberries
1 cup blueberries or substitute black & red raspberries
1/4 cup maple syrup

Orange Juice Sauce

A semi-sweet healthful topping for toast, pancakes or french toast. Great topping for ice cream, too.

1 cup fresh orange juice (frozen may be used)
1 large peeled & seeded orange, chopped to small bits
2 teaspoons corn starch
2 tablespoons maple syrup
Dash almond extract

Heat maple syrup and orange juice in a sauce pan over low heat. Stir in corn starch to thicken. When mixture is near boiling, add almond extract. Stir and boil for a few minutes. Pour in orange bits and allow to simmer for five minutes.

When sauce thickens, remove and use as topping. Serve surrounded by sliced navel oranges.

Breakfast

If You Miss Breakfast on the Road

Try dried fruit, nuts, sweets and even a few freeze dried foods as energy boosters. They require no preparation (eat-right-out-of-the-packet type). Don't forget granola, chocolate bits, raisins and beef jerky chews (see our recipe). And if you didn't have time for morning exercise, here are some on the road exercises.

A good way to reduce potential double chins is by lifting your chin slightly. Now open and close your mouth as when chewing. Be sure to keep your eyes on the road, though. Getting thick in the waist (a common problem for all of us) is helped by sitting straight with your back against the seat. Pull your stomach in while holding your breath for approximately five seconds. Relax and repeat again. Tension is reduced and this helps fight sleepiness.

Lunch

Seafood Salad Buffet

A main salad dish for setting out on the picnic table for an afternoon treat or a Friday seafood buffet.

2 pounds jumbo shrimp
    (medium, if on a budget)
1 pound lump crabmeat
2 large tins sardines in
    tomato sauce
2 pints cherry tomatoes
2 cups bulgur wheat
4 tablespoons olive oil
1 tablespoon margarine
4 green onions, sliced
3/4 cup lemon juice
2 cups water
2 tablespoons parsley

Soak bulgur, lemon and water in large bowl. Boil shrimp and lemon in pan for five minutes (longer if frozen). Cool, peel and devein. Chop up half of the shrimp and combine with crabmeat and other ingredients in large salad bowl. Toss and mix together. In aluminum foil, chill and serve with remaining shrimp. Place sardines in another serving plate with a sliced lemon and saltine crackers. Create a shrimp dip with a mixture of two parts catsup to one part horseradish.

Another addition to the buffet: warm clam chowder soup (right out of the can).

Lunch

White Chicken Salad

A weight watcher's delight with plenty of protein. Enough to feed a half dozen or more.

4 cups white chicken, chopped
2 cups green grapes, seedless
2 eggs, hardboiled
1/2 head romaine lettuce
1/4 cup celery, chopped
1/2 cup mayonnaise
1 tablespoon parsley
Mint sprigs to garnish
Dash salt and pepper

To prepare, place chicken, grapes, celery, mayonnaise and parsley in a large bowl and stir. Tear lettuce into large pieces. Place the lettuce on a serving plate. Top with the chicken salad. Garnish the salad with sprigs of mint. Sprinkle with salt and pepper.

Garden Spinach Salad

Your vegetable requirements are all in this luncheon combination for at least six.

Salad
4 cups iceberg lettuce, torn
1 cup fresh spinach, torn
5 cherry tomatoes, halved
3 hardboiled eggs, sliced
1 small yellow onion, sliced
1/4 cup black olives, diced
4 radishes, sliced
Dash garlic powder

Homemade Dressing
1/4 cup white wine vinegar
1/4 cup vegetable oil
2 tablespoons barbecue sauce
1/4 teaspoon salt
Dash pepper

Combine all salad ingredients in a salad serving bowl. In another (small) bowl, blend the dressing ingredients. Toss salad and pour dressing over to taste.

Lunch

Cherry Gelatin Salad

For about 12 servings — all you need are some Bing cherries, water, gelatin and two molds (1-quart size)

> 1 cup Bing cherries
> 1 teaspoon sugar
> 1 six ounce package cherry flavored
>   gelatin
> 2 cups boiling water
> 2 cups cold water
> 3 ounce walnuts or pecans,
>   chopped (optional)
> Spurt of whipping cream for each serving
>   (optional)
> Note: For six servings use one mold
> (1-quart size), reduce ingredients
> one-half

Empty the package of gelatin in a bowl. Stir in two cups of very hot water. Blend in the sugar and add two cups of cold water. Pour contents into a large bowl and chill. Spray the molds with non-stick oil. As gelatin thickens add the pitted cherries. Pour mixture into the prepared molds. Chill until firm. Unmold and serve topped with whipping cream and walnuts/pecans.

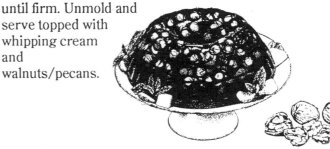

Mother's Potato Salads

What would an outdoor picnic be without the choice of either cold or hot potato salads?

Chilled:
8 red potatoes
4 eggs, hardboiled
1 celery stalk, chopped
1 yellow onion, finely
  chopped
1 teaspoon salt
1 tablespoon parsley, chopped
1/2 cup mayonnaise
Squirt yellow mustard
Dash pepper

Boil potatoes 20 to 30 minutes, peel and cube. Shell, slice and toss eggs in with potatoes in a large bowl. Add the rest of the ingredients and toss lightly. Blend the mayonnaise into the salad with the mustard. Chill before serving. Mother suggests: serve with boiled ham, egg salad in whites, rye bread and mustard on the side.

Hot:
8 red potatoes
1 pound lean bacon, diced
  (low salt)
2 tablespoons brown sugar
1/2 cup vinegar (cider)
1 yellow onion, finely chopped
1/2 teaspoon salt
Dash pepper
Dash red pepper (optional)
A touch of beer (optional)

Boil potatoes for 20 to 30 minutes, peel and slice. Place in bowl. Pan-fry diced bacon and remove from pan. In the bacon drippings, add onions and cook until tender. Stir in sugar, vinegar (beer), salt and peppers. Heat this sauce to boiling, stirring often. Add diced bacon pieces to the sauce and pour over potatoes in serving bowl. Smooth sauce evenly on the sliced potatoes. Serve while hot. Mother also suggests: serve with beer-battered lake perch.

Lunch

Egg Salad in Whites

**6 eggs, extra large
1/4 cup mayonnaise
1/2 yellow onion, finely
    chopped
Squirt of yellow mustard
Dash salt and pepper**

Hardboil the eggs, shell and slice in half. Remove and mix yolks with other ingredients. Repack whites with yolk mixture. Sprinkle with paprika and chill.

Door County Cider Applesauce

Here's another idea for those fresh-picked apples. A cider apple-sauce that adds spice to a Door County fish boil
(see recipe).

**8 cups apples, peeled and
    diced**

**1/4 cup brown sugar
2 cups apple cider**

You'll need a blender for the diced apples. Place on low to medium speed with all the ingredients. In a sauce pan, boil the mixture, cover and simmer another 15 minutes. This recipe is also ideal for canning. A little dash of cinnamon might be added for a spicier taste.

Huge 'Texas' Burgers & Sliced Cheese Spuds

Burgers with a blend of herbs and spices. Broil in a covered cooker or fry in our 10-inch cast iron skillet and cover to hold in juices.

**1 pound ground chuck
1 cup bread crumbs
1 teaspoon garlic powder
3 beaten eggs
1 tablespoon chili
    powder
1 teaspoon ground
    cumin
2 teaspoon salt
1 tablespoon parsley,
    chopped
3 hot peppers, chopped and
    seeds removed (optional)**

Mix all ingredients, blending well. Shape into thick burgers and brown in butter on each side with top on. Cook over low fire or simmer for ten minutes.

Sliced Cheese Spuds (Potatoes)

A mouth-watering delight standing on its own merits. After rinsing baking potatoes, cut them into slices approximately halfway through. Mix up a cup of: salt, chives, parsley, garlic powder and grated cheddar cheese. Allow one tablespoon per potato of the above ingredients. If your tastes run spicy, add cumin, thyme and sage (one tsp. per potato) Pour melted butter or margarine over sliced pieces and sprinkle seasonings from cup over buttered area. Wrap potatoes individually in aluminum foil. Place on grate over a red hot coal fire. Cook for 50 minutes (adding coals) and turn often. Cut open top of foil and add 1/2 slice of cheddar cheese. Cook until soft inside. Start your Texas burgers after adding cheese. Serve burgers and spuds with a tall beverage.

Lunch

Banana Bacon on Buns

Baked bananas with bacon rolled around — served on heated hot dog buns. An unusual taste experience. Try it — you'll like it!

6 firm bananas, peeled
6 strips bacon (low salt)
6 oat bran hot dog buns
1 tablespoon margarine
Dash chopped parsley

Precook bacon until it begins to become firm. Wrap bacon around bananas and place on margarine brushed aluminum foil. Hold bacon on with toothpicks. Place foil over grate (middle of fire). Cover and bake until bananas are lightly brown and tender to a fork. Remove toothpicks. Sprinkle with parsley and serve on warmed oat bran hot dog buns.

Hobo Ham Stew

It gets better and better as you simmer and stir. Keep the lid on over a low fire. When you're camping for a full day, start your stew early in the morning. You'll be tempted by its savory smell to sample a cup at noon. Every time you warm it up, you'll enjoy it more. Our basic ingredients are leftovers from a precooked shank or butt ham and plenty of fresh or frozen vegetables.

Take the remaining whole ham and drop into a kettle of water (6-quart pan). Cook until the ham is tender enough to fall off the bone. Remove the ham from the beginnings of your stew. Discard bone and return ham pieces to the simmering water. Add onions, celery, carrots, potatoes and cabbage.

For seasoning, stir in:
1 tablespoon salt
1 teaspoon black pepper
1 tablespoon oregano
2 tablespoons garlic powder
2 tablespoons brown sugar
Sprinkle of ground cloves

For extra flavor, add a touch of pineapple juice, ginger ale and tomato sauce. Continue to simmer, stirring occasionally for about 40 minutes. At this time, frozen green beans and corn may be added. Serve with thick bread for dipping in the soup.

Hobo ham stew – an inexpensive meal that warms the stomach at twilight. And, you might even hear a train whistle in the distance when sipping and dipping.

Lunch

Campfire Chili

My special recipe for a warm (to hot) lunch is easy to make, feeds many, and grows stronger every time it's warmed up. You will need a good cast iron kettle and cover that can be placed over a wood fire for cooking the meat and later an ember fire to simmer adding flavor and a pleasing aroma to the campsite.

To start, use olive oil as a base for the cast iron cooking pot. Start to heat the kettle after placing on a metal grill (grate) over the hot fire. Add approximately four pounds of lean ground beef. Constantly stir meat until it starts to gray. Now add fresh water (about 4 cups). Let your fire die down to embers. Cook with top on for 30 minutes. You can scoop off some grease occasionally. In the meantime, peel, cut and add two yellow onions. In a small bowl, mix up the spices.

3 tablespoons chili powder
1 teaspoon cumin
4 bay leaves (remove before eating)
1 teaspoon oregano
1 tablespoon garlic powder
1 teaspoon sugar
1 teaspoon black pepper
   (you may add red pepper if another "fire" is desired)
1-2 teaspoons salt
   (depends on blood pressure)
Smidgen of seasoned salt
1 small can of tomato sauce (optional)
1 can pinto beans or kidney beans
   (optional) — remember, you are outdoors

Add all of these ingredients when the fire becomes low, stir often for at least an hour. To thicken, add a cup of watered corn starch or flour. Be sure to keep lid on. Serve with crackers, tacos or corn chips.

Italian Style Sub

A loaf of fresh Italian bread goes a long way on a trip if it's turned into a submarine sandwich. Here's our version. Slice a full-size loaf of Italian bread from end to end (cut halfway down). Fill generously with the following meats: 97 percent fat-free ham (sliced extra thin), turkey breast (sliced extra thin), beef bologna (sliced extra thin). Salami is optional. Add lettuce, sliced tomatoes, diced onions, black olives, shredded cheeses (your choice), sweet and sour sliced pickles. Pour on all ingredients with oil and vinegar mixture. Sprinkle with Parmesan cheese (oregano optional).

Lunch

French Style Pizza

A loaf of fresh French bread becomes two pizzas when sliced from end to end into halves. Cover both flat sides with pizza sauce or seasoned spaghetti sauce. Add strips of mozzarella cheese (muenster cheese can be substituted). Here's where it gets different. One half of the bread pizza will be cheese only. The other half becomes "the works." Cover it with pepperoni, diced ham, precooked or smoked sausage slices (or both). The extras can include mushrooms, green or black olives, sliced onions, canned shrimp, green peppers and both Swiss & cheddar cheese. Wrap each half in greased aluminum foil. Place on grill over low fire. Turn over deep pan and cover the bread to reflect heat from the grill. Cut both of these bread stuffers into generous portions. Warm until cheese melts. Your "customers" will be back for seconds.

Dinner

In a covered cooker, place a square roasting pan with hot charcoal on each side. We recommend this method of charcoal placement for the following three family recipes. Always wrap the whole pan with aluminum foil to hold flavor and juices (also protects pan). Keep top of cooker on. Open all cooker holes.

Dinner

Burgundy Roast Beef

We prefer a sirloin tip (although rump is fine). Usually five to six lbs. and rolled boneless. Peeled potatoes, halved (your choice); yellow onions, peeled. Whole carrots and fresh mushrooms (do not pick outdoors) surround the roast. Cover contents with 1/2 cup of dry Burgundy wine. On roast sprinkle salt, pepper, thyme, garlic powder and parsley to your own tastes. Depending on weight, we cook a minimum of $1^1/2$ hours. Add coals on each side if fire cools down. Gravy can be made from the natural juices and remaining wine flavor. Thicken with flour.

Stuffed Turkey Breast

There are two reasons for the popularity of this recipe in our family. Everyone prefers white meat and everyone likes pork sausage in the dressing. The best for our purposes is sage sausage bulk in a roll. We precook in an iron skillet the whole pound of sausage till it's almost browned. We only use approximately 1/2. The remainder is put aside for a topping for an outdoor pizza snack. The sage sausage is added to a bowl of whole wheat bread bits and pieces (six to eight slices), 1/2 cup of chopped yellow onions and one teaspoon of poultry seasoning. Mix together and stuff the cavity after washing out and salting the inside. Place the stuffed turkey breast (bone in) in a square baking pan. Cover totally with double-strength aluminum foil and place in the cooker with red hot coals on both sides of the cooking pan. Allow $3^1/2$ hours or more and check the thermometer or poke fork in the thickest part. If the fork pushes in easily, meat is cooked. Remember to add coals every hour or so. You'll find the pan full of juices for gravy. Just thicken these juices with flour. The turkey is always very tender and moist from this method of cooking.

Dinner

Barbecued Country Ribs & Chicken

Our secret ingredient is the spicy sauce. We hope you like its bite!

Barbecue Sauce
1/4 cup brown sugar
1 tablespoon catsup
1/4 cup tomato paste
1 tablespoon chili powder
1/2 cup worcestershire sauce
1 tablespoon dry mustard
1 teaspoon salt
1/2 cup granulated sugar
1 cube beef bouillon
1/4 cup white wine (Rhine)
1/4 cup white vinegar
2 tablespoons yellow onion, chopped
1 tablespoon garlic powder
1 dash tabasco

Combine all the ingredients and simmer in a sauce pan for approximately two hours. Do not cover. You may need to add water to prevent burning. Stir often. You should end up with one quart for ribs, chicken and more.

Country Ribs

We boil them in a large kettle in a mixture of ginger ale (12 ounces) and water for 45 minutes. This reduces the fat content and spices up the taste.

Country Chicken

In the meantime, our chicken breasts and legs (with skin removed) are baked or fried in white wine (Rhine) for 30 minutes. We take mixed frozen vegetables and add in the wine sauce surrounding the chicken and simmer for another 15 minutes.

We're now ready to remove the fully cooked country ribs and chicken and place them on the grill while pouring our spicy barbecue sauce on. A very low charcoal fire is best. Excessive fire or heat destroys the sugar in the sauce. Continue to cook no longer than 15 minutes. You may want to diffuse the heat with aluminum foil on the grill. Be sure to cover the cooker and remember to serve the vegetables in the wine sauce. Feature garlic bread with your country ribs and chicken fest.

Ethnic

Greek Saganaki Appetizer

Flaming cheese famous in Greek restaurants along Halsted street in Chicago. It's this easy.

    1 pound Kasseri cheese
    3 tablespoons 2% milk
    3 eggs
    1 cup flour

Cut your cheese at least 1/4-inch thick. Mix eggs in milk, then dip the cheese in the blend and again in the flour. Pan fry in olive oil (use a wok skillet) until lightly browned. We don't recommend you flame with brandy. It can be dangerous.

Just add a touch of lemon (and brandy) when serving. Crusty Italian or French bread is best. Make a one-sided Saganaki sandwich. Serve with Roditis wine.

Russian Shrimp with Bloody Mary Mix Dip

The vodka is only enough to slightly intoxicate the shrimp.

    2 tablespoons 80 proof vodka
    1 pound large shrimp
    2 jiggers (shots) of Smooth & Spicy
        Bloody Mary Cocktail Mix
    1 tablespoon light soy sauce
    1 tablespoon garlic powder
    3 chopped green onions
    1 tablespoon salt
    1 tablespoon grated ginger
    1 tablespoon margarine

Marinate the shrimp in shells for ten minutes in vodka, ginger and soy sauce. Drain off. Over high heat, stir-fry shrimp (in shells) with vegetable oil and garlic. Add salt and onions. Stir until shrimp color is bright pink-orange. Now add Bloody Mary mix over contents. Put on lid and turn off heat. Serve while still hot.

Ethnic

Dutch Split Pea Soup

Hearty dish that warms the insides on a misty day. Serves eight big appetites.

2 cups dried green split peas
1/2 cup ham, diced
3 to 4 carrots, sliced
1 cup celery, chopped
1 teaspoon garlic powder
3 small peeled potatoes, diced
2 sweet spanish onions, chopped
6 cups water
2 teaspoons parsley
2 tablespoons peanut oil
2 tablespoons margarine
Dash bacon bits

Boil dried peas for two minutes. Cover and let stand for one hour. In a large pot place the oil and margarine with the onions and celery over a medium heat. As onions soften, stir in peas with garlic powder. Put in 6 cups of water and bring to boil. Cover and reduce heat. Simmer for 30 minutes. Potatoes and parsley should be added. Simmer for another 30 minutes until peas and potatoes thicken soup. Add an additional 1/2 cup of water if it becomes too thick.

If you enjoy more of a meaty flavor, add a ham bone or beef bone with meat when you warm up leftovers. Other extras to consider are a diced sweet potato and cherry tomatoes. Serve with croutons.

Scottish Stew with Dumplings

Start with a large iron kettle and a tight-fitting cover for this thrifty stew that goes a long way.

2 pounds boneless lamb (shoulder)
    sliced into 2-inch strips
1/4 cup flour
2 teaspoons salt
Dash pepper

Mix ingredients for breading. Bread lamb pieces and brown in oiled kettle on all sides. Add 1 quart of water and bring to boil. Simmer for another 1^1/2 hours.
    Add:
6 yellow onions, chopped
6 celery stalks, sliced
6 small carrots, sliced
8 red potatoes, sliced
2 teaspoons salt
Dash pepper, basil and marjoram

Simmer for another 45 minutes. Garnish with chopped parsley on generous servings.

Dumplings
3 cups flour
6 teaspoons baking powder
2 teaspoons salt
1 tablespoon vegetable shortening
1 cup 2% milk

Mix flour, baking powder and salt together. Add shortening while blending until it becomes textured. Add milk and continue to stir until just blended. After lamb and stew vegetables have cooked 30 minutes, lay dumplings on top of stew. Use a tablespoon carefully. Do not let the dumplings settle down in kettle. Pour off excess liquid to prevent this. Cover tightly and cook over medium heat for another 30 minutes. Sprinkle with parsley when serving.

Ethnic

Chinese Chop Suey with White Rice

Cantonese dishes always seem to go over big in the backwoods. The food is not heavy and goes a long way.

>3 pounds chicken breast, cut in small
>   cubes
>1 pound veal or beef
>2 yellow onions, sliced
>4 stalks celery, chopped
>1 can mushrooms, drained
>5 beef bouillon cubes, dissolved
>2 tablespoons soy sauce
>1 small green pepper, chopped
>1 can bean sprouts
>1 teaspoon brown sugar
>1 teaspoon salt
>Dash pepper

In a 6-quart kettle, brown meat in olive oil. Add onions and pepper and cook for 1/2 hour over medium fire. Add soy sauce, salt, brown sugar and beef bouillons. Simmer for 20 minutes with lid on.

Mix in mushrooms, celery, bean sprouts and dash of pepper. Cook another ten minutes. Eight to ten servings with rice. Don't forget the fortune cookies.

White Rice
To be sure of fluffy rice, always measure out. Add lemon to whiten rice.

>2 cups rice
>1 teaspoon salt
>1 teaspoon lemon juice
>1 beef bouillon

Drop rice into 4 cups of boiling salted water. Add a squirt of lemon juice. Boil quickly to prevent sticking until tender (approximately 20 minutes). Drain and serve steaming with chop suey.

Irish Corned Beef & Cabbage

>5 to 6 pounds corned beef brisket
>3 tablespoons garlic powder
>1 large yellow onion, chopped
>6 whole peppercorns
>6 whole allspice berries
>1 teaspoon salt
>3 bay leaves (remove when done)
>Dash parsley and pepper

Cook corned beef brisket in water to the boiling point in a 6-quart kettle. Stir in all the above ingredients. Add a touch of Irish stout for extra taste (optional). Simmer approximately four hours (40 minutes per pound).

Boiled Cabbage
Prepare during the last hour of corned beef preparation. Remove tough outside leaves and quarter the cabbage. Place in boiling salted water. Cook for 30 minutes until soft. Drain and season with margarine, garlic powder and pepper to taste.

Slice corned beef brisket into 1/4-1/2-inch slices and place over cabbage on a serving dish. Sprinkle with parsley. Serve with hot mustard sauce or horseradish on the side.

Ethnic

Celebration Chicken — Italian Style

Here's a bubbly version of "chicken cacciatore" with other extras. You need one fryer chicken cut up and extra chicken legs or breasts. Peel off skin and wash.

1/2 bottle Italian Spumante
1 small can tomato paste
1 teaspoon oregano
1 teaspoon salt
1 small can mushrooms
3 small yellow onions, sliced
3 small green peppers, chopped
    (seeds removed)
4 red potatoes, peeled and sliced (thick)
6 carrots, cleaned and sliced (thick)
1 teaspoon parsley
2 teaspoons garlic powder
2 bay leaves
Dash pepper
Touch of lemon (optional)

Heat large skillet with olive oil base to braise chicken-brown on all sides with high heat. Drain off oil and add the above mixed spices, tomato paste and vegetables on low heat. Pour Spumante over entire ingredients. Simmer with lid on for 45 minutes. Periodically pour on more Spumante. Remove lid to thicken sauce. Add water to thin. Serves four to six. A good choice for New Years!

Kielbasa and Kraut

Here's a dish at the border between Poland and Germany, that's strong in smell and taste. Other campers will notice this one.

4 pounds fresh or smoked polish
    sausage (we like both)
1 large can sauerkraut (fresh may
    be used)
2 apples grated
1/4 stick margarine
1/4 cup brown sugar
1 yellow onion, minced
Dash salt and pepper

Boil fresh sausage after adding half a bottle of imported beer. Cook for one hour. Smoked sausage does not have to be pre-cooked.

In a covered iron skillet, brown the sauerkraut in margarine adding minced onion, brown sugar and grated apples. Add dash of salt and pepper.

Stir ingredients in the remaining half bottle of beer. Top with either pre-cooked fresh sausage or smoked sausage after cutting into 4 to 5 -inch pieces. Cover and simmer for one hour. Serve with garlic bread.

Starting with a can

Corned Beef Hash Cakes Topped with a Poached Egg

An eye opener in the morning served on a buttered English muffin or with wheat toast. For four:

    1 medium-size can corned beef hash
    6 small eggs
    **1/2 cup 2% milk (water may be
        substituted)**
    1 teaspoon parsley
    Dash salt and pepper

Fill sauce pan with approximately 1-inch of milk (or water). Bring to boil. Carefully break eggs into a saucer. Slide one egg at a time into pan and cover. Simmer for three to five minutes.

In the meantime, prepare patties of hash in warm nonstick skillet. Top each with a poached egg. Sprinkle with parsley and pepper to taste.

Salmon Patties (or Loaf)

These delicious patties cook in minutes. The salmon loaf will require baking and, of course, additional time.

    2 large cans pink salmon, drained
    1/4 cup cracker crumbs
    1/4 cup oatmeal
    1 small yellow onion, finely chopped
    1 teaspoon salt
    1 tablespoon margarine
    Dash black pepper

Mix ingredients and form into patties (or loaf). Cook salmon patties with vegetable oil in large wok. Gently turn over after eight to ten minutes. Cook another five minutes. Salmon loaf should bake for one hour or more.

Serve with steamed peas and small onions (muffins if you are baking).

Starting with a can

Brats & Beans

Just combine a medium-size can of baked beans and a small tin of ham. Dice the ham and add to the baked beans while warming over a low fire in a non-stick skillet. The brats can be added to the pan or cooked directly over an open fire. Serve brats and beans together or top the brats in a bun with ham and bean mixture.

Chili-Dogs

Lean ground beef, chopped onions and peppers are fried in a nonstick skillet. A medium-size can of chili is added and stirred in for ten minutes. Hot dogs are warmed directly in the pan or roasted over an open fire. Serve chili and dogs together or top the hot dogs in a bun with this ground beef enriched chili.

Burger-Corn

This recipe was handed down from my dad, who was a Green Bay lumberjack at one time.

1 large can corn (green and red pepper blend)
1 pound ground chuck
1 teaspoon garlic powder
1 teaspoon salt
Dash pepper

Cook ground chuck in an oiled frying pan until it turns greyish. Stir in corn, garlic powder and salt. Cook over medium heat for ten minutes. Sprinkle with black pepper. Serve on warm wheat or oat bran buns with a touch of butter.

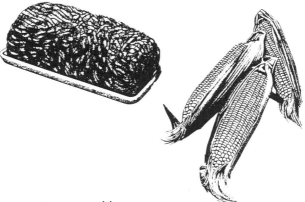

Starting with a box

Macaroni & Cheese Dogs

Serves four
Macaroni & cheese dinner
(7¹/4 ounce package)
4 turkey cheese dogs
1 teaspoon onions, minced
1 tablespoon catsup
1/4 cup half & half
1 teaspoon salt
4 tablespoons margarine
Dash pepper

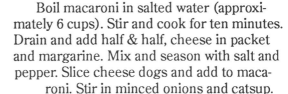

Boil macaroni in salted water (approximately 6 cups). Stir and cook for ten minutes. Drain and add half & half, cheese in packet and margarine. Mix and season with salt and pepper. Slice cheese dogs and add to macaroni. Stir in minced onions and catsup. Bake covered for another 30 minutes. Serve with warm garlic bread.

Mostaccioli & Meatballs

Serves six
Mostaccioli (1 pound package)
1 pound ground chuck
1 beaten egg
1/2 cup grated Romano cheese
1 quart spaghetti sauce with mushrooms
1/2 cup bread crumbs
1 teaspoon salt
2 tablespoons olive oil
1 teaspoon garlic powder
1/2 teaspoon ground oregano
Dash pepper

Prepare meatballs by combining the ground chuck with the beaten egg and bread crumbs. Stir in the grated cheese, salt, garlic powder, ground oregano and a sprinkle of pepper. Shape into meatballs. Brown meatballs in heated olive oil – coated skillet. Add sauce, cover pan and simmer for 30 minutes. Combine with mostaccioli.

Boil mostaccioli in salted water (approximately four quarts). Cook 15 minutes. Drain, add margarine and serve sauce and meatballs over and around mostaccioli. Serve with warm buttered garlic bread.

Starting with a box

Beef Taco Salsa Shells

Serves eight
Taco shells (1¼ ounce box)
1 pound ground chuck
Medium taco sauce (8 ounces)
Small head lettuce, shredded
1/4 pound cheddar cheese, grated
1/4 pound Swiss cheese, grated
4 cherry tomatoes, sliced
3/4 cup water
Touch of salsa
Pitted black olives (optional)
Onions, chopped (optional)
Sour cream (optional)

Brown ground chuck in a skillet until crumbly and drain fat. Add taco sauce, water and stir. Bring to a boil and simmer for 20 minutes. Place taco shells on cookie sheet, fill shells with approximately 3 tablespoons of meat sauce and bake for five minutes at 350°. Top each shell with cheeses, lettuce and tomatoes. Shredded chicken or turkey can be added for extra taste. Garnish with mild Mexican salsa.

Starting with a packet

Danny's Noodles

Our littlest guy's favorite is beef-flavored Ramen noodle soup, which is made simply by adding the packet's contents to 2 cups of boiling water in a 2-quart saucepan. Over medium heat, cook the noodles for approximately three minutes or until tender. Stir in contents of seasoning packet. A 3-ounce packet is good for two servings (Danny eats both). Precooked ground chuck can also be stirred in when serving for a main dish in minutes.

Snacks

Chicago Style Pizza Squares (or Slices)

You'll need the camp oven or a baking attachment over a burner for this 10- x 10- inch, loaded-with-extras, biscuit-based thick-crust pizza.

> 1 tube biscuit mix
> 1 large link Italian sausage
> 1 small stick of pepperoni, sliced thin
> 1/2 cup spaghetti sauce
> 8 mozzarella slices
> 1 small onion, chopped
> 1 small pepper, diced
> 1 small can mushrooms, drained
> 1 small can black olives, pitted and halved
> Dash pepper
> Dash garlic powder
> Dash oregano
> Sprinkle with Parmesan cheese

Precook Italian sausage in boiling water for 45 minutes. Follow directions for biscuit mix preparation. Grease pizza pan with margarine. Sprinkle dough base with flour and roll out on pan tucking edges. Should be approximately 1/4-inch thick with 1-inch ends. Spread spaghetti sauce over the dough and pile on vegetables — distributing evenly. Slice precooked sausage and crumble over pizza. Add thinly sliced pepperoni generously over the sausage bare areas. Cover the whole pizza with cheese pieces. Sprinkle all the seasonings on. Also sprinkle with Parmesan cheese for extra taste. Bake at 375° until base is golden and insides are cooked. Allow extra time for thicker crusts.

Cut into squares for snacks or slices for serious eating.

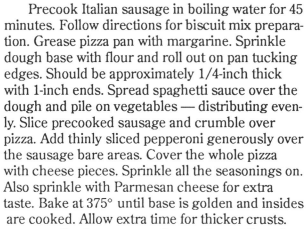

Beef Jerky Chews

These beef strips are easy to make, taste great, and save you a lot of money on snack costs at the store.

> 1-1/2 pounds thick Swiss steak, sliced (round steak will do)
> 3 tablespoons red Burgundy wine
> 1/4 cup soy sauce
> 1 tablespoon brown sugar
> 1 teaspoon catsup
> 1 teaspoon garlic powder
> 1 teaspoon onion salt
> 1 teaspoon sesame oil
> 1 teaspoon ginger
> Dash black pepper
> Dash chili powder
> Dash powdered mustard

Slice off in approximately 1/4-inch strips to lengths of 6 to 8 inches and marinate in the above mixed ingredients.

For those in a hurry…
Marinate for 30 to 45 minutes.
Broil on intense fire on just one side until browned.

The more natural way – Let the sun do the work.
Marinate overnight.
Dry on tray for 24 hours until water content is gone. Jerkies should be hard and dark before eating.

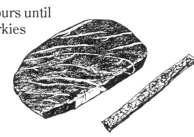

Snacks

Popcorn Balls

If you do not have an electric popper, the next best thing is a heavy skillet or wok featuring a tight-fitting cover. Oil the pan and add enough kernels to just layer the bottom. Cover tightly and shake over a medium heat. When popping stops, fill a large bowl (add salt) until you have 12 cups of popped corn

12 cups popped corn
1 teaspoon salt
1 cup brown sugar
1 cup corn syrup
1/2 cup half & half
1 teaspoon vinegar (cider)

Mix ingredients in a saucepan while stirring in the cream and syrup, slowly bringing to a boil. Keep stirring until syrup thickens (few minutes). Pour hot syrup over popcorn. With large spoon, stir and coat popcorn. As it cools press the popcorn with margarine-coated hands in 20 firm balls.

Double-Dip Fudge Apples with Nuts

Here's what to do with those fresh apples you are picking in the fall. Insert wooden picks in the apple cores, after washing. Be sure to dry thoroughly before dipping.

8 to 10 apples
8 (1 ounce) semisweet chocolate
    squares (Baker)
8 to 10 wooden picks
1-1/2 sticks margarine or
    unsalted butter
1 cup whipping cream
    (1 cup evaporated
    milk may be substituted)
1-1/2 cups nuts, chopped
1 cup sugar
2/3 cup corn syrup
1 tablespoon vanilla

In a sauce pan bring margarine, cream, corn syrup and sugar to a full boil, stirring often until sugar dissolves. Stir in vanilla and add chocolate squares and peanuts. Mix well. Continue stirring briskly until sauce is smooth. Pour into deep bowl quickly.

Double dip apples into fudge and let stand on wax paper or chill until firm. You'll have no trouble getting someone to "clean" the dipping pan.

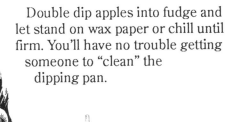

Drinks

Coffee 'For Adults Only'

When camping out on a cold night, nothing beats Irish coffee in a steamed goblet or heavy duty coffee mug. It's not bad in an army canteen cup, either. It can be made with Irish whiskey or good old-fashioned American bourbon. I know an Irish person who likes his with Scotch whiskey. Our formula for mentally beating the chill:

All of these ingredients come together, except the cream is added last. Be sure to drink the hot mixture through the cold thick cream. You'll know it's done right by checking out the moustaches around the wood fire.

    1 teaspoon fine sugar
    3/4 cup strong hot coffee (decaf can
       be used)
    1 ounce whiskey (your choice)
    1 small can heavy thick cream (whipping
       cream may be substituted)

Fruit Thirst Quencher

Old fashioned lemonade just like grandmother used to make — a full 2 quarts of refreshing energy.

    6 lemons
    8 cups cool water
    5 tablespoons honey

Squeeze the lemons for the juice. Place the lemon juice, water and honey in a 2-quart container. Stir or shake before serving. Add ice to cups or glasses and serve.

Drinks

Natural Fruit Soda

Nothing artificial in these ingredients. Any fruit juice mixed with sparkling natural water will do. Apple, pineapple, orange or cherry juices are fine. Just mix half and half.

Add berries for extra flavor. Kids will love these natural drinks served with ice.

A Special Recipe For Extra Taste and Enjoyment

When those mouth-watering smells filter through the campsite, keep your fellow campers in mind. Many of our best meals have been shared in potluck get-togethers. It's part of our heritage since colonial times to create a menu of shared potluck. Someone always makes great potato salad, a wild rice casserole or wants you to try some deer meat sausage. Add some ethnic food such as Mexican style tortilla cheese wrap-ups, and your taste buds are given a 10-course workout. Congenial hospitality and laughter makes a potluck get-together good for the digestive system. It's also a great way to add new recipes to your campout kitchen. Invite your neighbors over for a shared potluck get-together.

47

Outdoor Recipe Ingredient Checklist

Fresh Meats
- ☐ Ground chuck
- ☐ Brats
- ☐ Cheese dogs (turkey)
- ☐ Ham shank or butt
- ☐ Sausage (smoked and fresh)
- ☐ Italian sausage
- ☐ Pork sausage
- ☐ Sage sausage
- ☐ Bacon (low salt)
- ☐ Turkey breast (bone in)
- ☐ Roast beef, sirloin tip (rolled)
- ☐ Swiss steak (or round)
- ☐ Fryer chicken (extra breasts and legs)
- ☐ Country ribs
- ☐ Boneless lamb
- ☐ Corned beef brisket

Canned Meats
- ☐ Corned beef hash
- ☐ Roast beef hash
- ☐ Chili (with meat)
- ☐ Meatballs
- ☐ Ham (97% fat free)
- ☐ Chopped chicken

Seafood
- ☐ Shrimp (medium)
- ☐ Lump crabmeat
- ☐ Smelt
- ☐ Lake perch
- ☐ White fish
- ☐ Trout/coho
- ☐ Sardines (canned)
- ☐ Pink salmon (large cans)

Sliced meats
- ☐ Turkey breast
- ☐ Beef bologna
- ☐ Salami
- ☐ Ham (97% fat free)
- ☐ Pepperoni

Vegetables
- ☐ Lettuce (iceburg and romaine)
- ☐ Potatoes (red and baking)
- ☐ Onions (yellow)
- ☐ Rice (Spanish)
- ☐ Sauerkraut cabbage
- ☐ Tomatoes (cherry)
- ☐ Beans (pinto)
- ☐ Beans (kidney)
- ☐ Split peas
- ☐ Carrots
- ☐ Corn (mixed)
- ☐ Mushrooms
- ☐ Celery
- ☐ Green peppers
- ☐ Hot peppers
- ☐ Bean sprouts
- ☐ Radishes
- ☐ Spinach
- ☐ Olives (green and black)
- ☐ Pickles (sour and kosher)

Breads and Pastas, etc.
- ☐ Oat bran bread
- ☐ Whole wheat bread
- ☐ French & Italian bread
- ☐ Hamburger buns (wheat)
- ☐ Hot dog buns (wheat)
- ☐ Muffins (English)
- ☐ Crackers/Saltines
- ☐ Biscuit mix
- ☐ Bulgur wheat
- ☐ Instant Ramen noodles
- ☐ Noodles
- ☐ Mostaccioli
- ☐ Taco shells
- ☐ Corn chips

Dairy Products
- ☐ Eggs
- ☐ Egg Substitutes
- ☐ Milk (2%)
- ☐ Cheeses (shredded)
- ☐ Cheese (Kasseri)
- ☐ Cheese (Romano)
- ☐ Half & half
- ☐ Whipping cream
- ☐ Evaporated milk
- ☐ Powdered eggs & milk

Frying and Baking Supplies
- ☐ Margarine
- ☐ Olive oil
- ☐ Vegetable shortening
- ☐ Sesame oil
- ☐ All- purpose flour
- ☐ Wheat flour
- ☐ Corn starch
- ☐ Seasoned breading
- ☐ Oatmeal
- ☐ Bread crumbs
- ☐ Baking powder
- ☐ Yeast

Seasonings/Flavorings
- ☐ Salt
- ☐ Black pepper
- ☐ Red pepper
- ☐ Sugar (all types)
- ☐ Oregano
- ☐ Bay leaves
- ☐ Onion salt
- ☐ Allspice berries
- ☐ Garlic powder
- ☐ Parsley
- ☐ Paprika
- ☐ Peppercorns (whole)
- ☐ Basil
- ☐ Grated ginger
- ☐ Chili powder
- ☐ Cumin
- ☐ Cloves
- ☐ Marjoram
- ☐ Poultry seasoning
- ☐ Sage
- ☐ Cinnamon
- ☐ Nutmeg
- ☐ Vanilla
- ☐ Almond extract
- ☐ Mint sprigs
- ☐ Dry mustard
- ☐ Beef bouillon cubes
- ☐ Chicken bouillon cubes

Toppings/Dressings
- ☐ Salad oils
- ☐ Italian dressing
- ☐ Vinegar (cider)
- ☐ White wine vinegar
- ☐ Mayonnaise
- ☐ Tomato sauce/paste
- ☐ Worcestershire sauce
- ☐ Taco sauce
- ☐ Salsa/tabasco sauce
- ☐ Barbecue sauce
- ☐ Spaghetti sauce
- ☐ Horseradish
- ☐ Catsup
- ☐ Mustard (yellow)

"Taste Touches"
- ☐ German & domestic beer
- ☐ Russian vodka
- ☐ Italian Spumante
- ☐ Rhine wine
- ☐ Burgundy wine
- ☐ Irish whiskey
- ☐ Bloody Mary mix
- ☐ Natural water

Sweets/Nuts
- ☐ Honey
- ☐ Corn syrup
- ☐ Maple syrup
- ☐ Sugar (brown)
- ☐ Chocolate bits
- ☐ Baking chocolate squares (semi-sweet)
- ☐ Walnuts
- ☐ Pecans
- ☐ Peanuts

Other
- ☐ Gelatin
- ☐ Fortune cookies
- ☐ Popcorn
- ☐ Wooden picks

Don't forget (if applicable)
- ☐ Baby food
- ☐ Dog food

Most of these ingredients are used in the recipes in this part.

PART V

Tips on Catching, Cleaning and Cooking Fish

Our son, James, in partnership with our Door County neighbor, Lynn, landed this contest winner — a Northern Pike in a channel located near Sturgeon Bay, Wisconsin

O n any camping trip, always plan on taking the fishing line along. There's probably water around somewhere, and nothing beats fresh fish cooked in the great outdoors. For the kids, there's always a fresh-cut willow or birch pole that can be instantly fashioned with some extra test line and hooks. Here are some natural fishing tips we've learned over a period of time.

Times to Fish

Usually fish feed just before dawn and right after dusk. Just before a storm and when the moon is full are excellent times to fish. Watch for jumping minnows as a sign of activity, too.

Where to fish

In lakes and larger streams, your choice should be near the bank and shallows, both in the morning and evening. In shallow streams, especially during hot weather, fish like to get together in the deepest part where it's cool. You'll find them under rocks and where underground water goes into the main-stream.

In deeper streams, fish

look for calmer water found around submerged rocks and logs. Check out the shaded areas provided by overhanging bushes and tree limbs. Another shelter is under deep undercut banks or at mouths of main rivers or streams that are high and very muddy. Observe what the fish are eating. Crabs, fish eggs, minnows or worms and insects on the bank. This should be your bait.

Fishing in the Winter

Try ice fishing for year-round fun, but be careful about frostbite and thin ice.

Target your catch

As a precaution when you are not familiar with the ice thickness, carry a 10-foot pole that's at least three-inches in diameter extended across your body. If the ice breaks under you you can still hold on to this extended pole and climb out.

Keep in mind when setting up your shanty on secure ice that fish tend to gather in shallow water in the winter. Projecting ice formations and shelves near shore drop-offs to the lake bottom are the best areas to start with. Remember to dress warm.

How to Target and Catch Fish

It's a known fact that fish occupy only about 10 percent of the total available water acreage. Today's fisher has to know a little about what's happening beneath the water's surface. Streams are very difficult to read because of the current flow and varying depth. The fish have favorites, too. Every species of fish has a special place in a certain type of pond, lake or stream. As an example, a stream may contain three types of trout — brown, brook and rainbow. It's a warm day and you're out early. The insect activity is nil. The water is clear, the sun bright and the stream level is normal. Upstream is where it's known the brown trout live and feed. However, they aren't interested in feeding until late afternoon or evening. In the meantime, it's a good idea to target brook trout.

The Right Lure for Brooks

Check the banks first. A lot of times it's "ants by the banks" at lunchtime.

Sometimes caught fish will reveal their choices when you clean them. Choose a lure that resembles their taste for the day. Brooks prefer the slowest moving streams. They are found in shaded pocket waters (70 degrees or less) behind large boulders.

Later in the afternoon, switch to brown trout because they like the deeper water and current that furnishes food opportunities. You'll find these hearty fish in cool turbulent flows during the summer. They also like streams that tend to warm up during the day.

If there's time later in the day, watch the rainbow trout activity. Rainbows are known to move about where there is plenty of oxygen available.

Think Like a Fish

To target fish you must study and learn their needs and habits. You should take time to read the waters by traveling up

and down the streams at different hours. At all times keep in mind that temperature, depth, current speed, cover, food, oxygen, bait and lures are choices affecting the type of fish you'll share at supper.

Fly Fishing

An excellent book on fly fishing is available from Sierra Outdoor Products (see the reference for details).

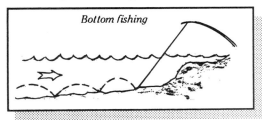

And, if you are successful, remember to keep your catches cool. If ice is not available, burlap bags, newspapers, moss or materials that "breathe" help preserve fish. Keep the covering moist.

Brown, Boat and Bottom Fishing Suggestions

Brown Trout Fishing. The German brown trout, a European import, is now the most widely distributed trout, and this trout is a survivor. It's definitely the toughest trout to catch and seems to thrive in most waters across the country. A tip: Use less colorful and smaller flys. Also, your chances are better at night. You'll have plenty of opportunities if you fish for browns in the Door County area around Sturgeon Bay.

Boat Fishing. In the back of a moving craft, troll an artificial lure (small spinner for perch) and let out the line 15 to 20 yards. Wobble your lure and cruise or row until you have a strike. You can also drop anchor and cast lures (or switch to live bait). Use large minnows for bass, small minnows for yellow perch, and hope for a school.

Bottom Fishing. Use a heavier sinker and one or more hooks with live bait. Walk it along the bottom, keeping the line tight. Keep your eyes on the rod tip for feeding fish.

Bottom fishing

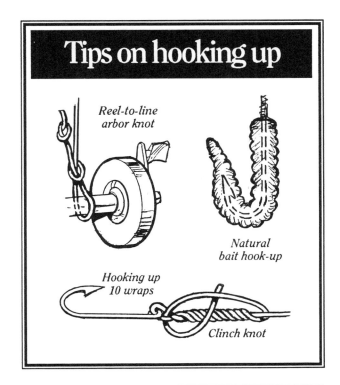

Tips on hooking up

Reel-to-line arbor knot

Natural bait hook-up

Hooking up 10 wraps

Clinch knot

Basic Fishing Gear Checklist

☐ Telescoping rod (or four section rod) and case

☐ Spinning reel

☐ Test lines (two and four pounds or stronger)

☐ #12 and 14 hooks (for small and large fish)

☐ Lures, assorted

☐ Weights, assorted

☐ Bait: worms, cheeses, hot dog pieces, insects, crabs and fish eggs where available

☐ A net for your catches

☐ Fishing license if required

Cleaning and Filleting the Catch

The easiest and quickest method for filleting is illustrated below. We recommend that the thin strip of fatty belly flesh on oily fish (salmon and large trout) be removed. Contaminants settle into this fatty tissue. You may also want to skin your fillet.

FILLETING

Step 1
Lift pectoral fin. Angle knife towards back of head. Cut to the backbone.

Step 4
Cut off the strip of fatty belly flesh. (Discard belly contents)

Step 2
Turn blade parallel to backbone. Cut towards tail with a sawing motion. Remove fillet.

Step 5
Cut into tail flesh to the skin. Turn blade parallel.

Step 3
Slide blade along rib bones for removal. Turn over fish and repeat procedure.

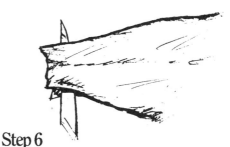

Step 6
Hold skin firmly while slicing in a sawing action between skin and flesh. Discard leftovers. To clean fillets, rinse under cold water and dry with paper towels.

Pan Dressing

Small fish such as yellow perch, bluegills and crappies are often too small for filleting. It's easy to pan-dress fish, (as illustrated).

1. **Scale, remove fins.**
2. **Open belly, clean out.**
3. **Remove head and tail.**
4. **Wash well.**

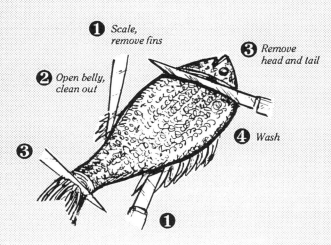

❶ *Scale, remove fins*

❷ *Open belly, clean out*

❸ *Remove head and tail*

❹ *Wash*

To freeze:

Give them a 30-second dip in a solution made up of two-thirds cup salt to one gallon of water. Then wrap and freeze.

Cooking Fish

Pan Frying the Catch

When the smelt season is on, this is the way we like them.

1 egg
1 cup flour
1 teaspoon garlic powder
1 teaspoon seasoned salt
Touch of lemon
Dash pepper

Use plenty of vegetable oil or margarine. Bring your heavy skillet to a sizzling state. Most fish require only minutes to cook. They should be turned over only once. Do not overcook. Breading tip: Use a small bag (lunch size) to bread your fillets. Add seasoning and flour or breading mix to the bag, dip the fish (no more than two at a time) in an egg/lemon batter (beer can be added). Place in the bag, shake briskly, and remove to sizzling pan. Repeat until all the fish or ingredients are gone. Keep your pan deep in the cooking oil, but do not drown the fish in the skillet. This makes the fish soggy. Fish skin should be crisp and brown. Cook fish approximately five to ten minutes. Drain on paper towels. Yum!

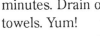

Cooking Fish

How to Deep-Fry the Catch

| Step 1 | Step 2 | Step 3 |
| Coat perch in mix. | Deep-fry at 375°. | Golden brown in minutes. |

Beer Batter Lake Perch

• •

The deep-fryer belonged to my father and so does this beer-flavored perch recipe that's best in March.

Use corn, peanut, or cottonseed oil, because they do not change or affect the flavor of fish. The secret to success is 375° proper oil temperature. If you're not using a deep fryer, then you always want bubbles when fish are added. Add no more than four at a time.

    1 egg
    1 cup flour
    7 ounces nonalcoholic beer
    1 teaspoon salt
    1 teaspoon garlic powder
    Dash pepper

Blend egg and beer in medium bowl. Mix flour, garlic powder, salt and pepper in brown lunch bag. Dip perch into egg and beer mix. Shake perch in bag until coated. Deep fry for three to four minutes until golden brown outside, crisp and flaky inside. Repeat ingredients for next batch.

Use the vegetable oil no more than two times. Strain oil through cheesecloth before using second time.

Cooking Fish

How to Grill Mouth-Watering Fish

For a moist texture, whole fish should be grilled with the heads and skin on. They can be removed later just before serving. Always grill fish approximately 5 to-6 inches from the fire or hot coals. A rule of thumb is ten minutes per inch of thickness. Fish steaks should be cut to 1-inch thickness for even and uniform grilling. Some flatfish types such as sole can be cooked without turning if using a cooker cover or foil wrapping. An ideal topping is a mix of bread crumbs, mustard, chopped scallions and a touch of lemon. Spread over after removing skin. Also sprinkle with paprika.

Charcoal-Grilled Whitefish and/or Trout

Using a covered cooker with good-sized filleted fish wrapped in aluminum foil provides a break from fried foods.

**6 filleted sides of whitefish
or trout (or both)
1 teaspoon olive oil
1 teaspoon garlic powder
1/2 lemon (juices)
1 teaspoon parsley
1 teaspoon oregano
1 tablespoon seasoned salt
Dash paprika
Dash pepper**

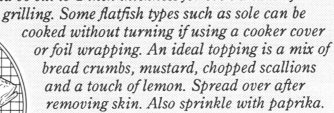

Heat your charcoal until white. Combine 1 tablespoon of olive oil, juice of 1/2 lemon, salt and pepper to taste (some garlic powder for those who do not worry about their breath), 1 teaspoon of oregano and 1 teaspoon of parsley. Spoon on both sides of fish. Wrap in foil. Cook on one side approximately seven minutes. Turn over and cook an additional seven minutes. Serve with remaining sauce on top. Sprinkle with paprika and pepper when serving. This method of cooking is also ideal for red snapper, bluefish or mackerel.

55

Sauces for the Catch

Tartar Sauce

Best when cooled for over four hours.

1 cup mayonnaise
1 teaspoon minced onion
3 tablespoon sweet/sour pickle,
chopped finely
1 tablespoon vinegar
1 tablespoon minced parsley
Dash white pepper

Mix all ingredients and refrigerate. Serve in paper cups.

Dill Sauce

Great with all fish and vegetables.

1 pint plain yogurt
3/4 cup mayonnaise
1 tablespoon minced onion
1/2 teaspoon lemon juice
1/2 teaspoon garlic powder
1 teaspoon dill weed
1 teaspoon fresh dill
Dash white pepper

Mix all ingredients. Refrigerate and serve with raw vegetables and dill pickles.

Horseradish Sauce

Recommended with broiled fish and baked Idaho potatoes.

3 tablespoons mild horseradish
1/2 cup sour cream
1 teaspoon garlic powder
4 black olives, chopped fine
1 teaspoon lemon juice
Dash salt and pepper
Touch dry white wine (optional)

Other toppings to add are:
Melted and browned margarine combined with one or more of:
Chives-mince and stir in
Onions-mince, stir in and cook until tender
Tabasco-a few drops stirred in
Worcestershire — 1/2 teaspoon stirred in
Lemon/lime — 1/2 teaspoon goes a long way

All of these sauces bring out the best in fresh seafood without burying the natural and delightful taste of just-caught fish. Try them all.

56

PART VI

Outdoor Living and Activity

Left: Exploring is a big part of our children's activities.
Below: The author and his wife stand at "Morning formation of family."

How to Survive Camping Out with 16 Kids

I t's really easy, if you can keep them busy and looking forward to the next activity planned. When we are on the road, everyone is looking forward to when and where we are stopping for a picnic lunch. Later, it's a special dinner or sometimes it's an unscheduled stop at a farm. After arriving, we try to get a game going — whether it's tossing a football, hitting out a few balls, or just tossing some frisbees.

"Making new friends"

Discoveries are common.

Main Meal Is Now Ready

Once all the chores are done, it's time to clean up and get ready for one of our special dinner recipes. After chow, everyone is on their own time to relax. Some read, some explore, others meet neighbor campers. Later, everyone is ready for a campfire. The tepee fire is started with folded newspapers and twigs. This becomes a great focal point for joking and storytelling. Some tall tales come from the smallest people. As the night rolls on, the stories become a little more frightening. Marshmallows are passed out, and last call is made for weiners and smoked sausage roasted over the late fire. Then lights and fire are put out and all gets quiet.

Discoveries Come First

After arriving there's always a few wanting to check out the campsite and its surroundings.

Later, at the campsite, everyone gets involved setting up the camp and unpacking. Gathering wood, twigs, etc., keeps the little guys busy and helps work up an appetite.

On a windy day, most of our older kids take out the kites. Burgers and dogs are started while cold cuts, potato salad, hardboiled eggs and casseroles are being set up. A variety of cool refreshments are available, too.

The end of day one.

Second Day Starts

After a hearty family breakfast of blueberry pancakes, scrambled eggs, sausage patties and loads of wheat toast, the next day's serious activities start. Some weight lifters start with a test of strength right at the breakfast table.

They are then encouraged to use their energies elsewhere with cycling, backpacking, canoeing, swimming, fishing and cycling (if bikes are available). In the winter, it's hockey, snowmobiling and cross-country skiing. Lunch is packed. Finally, everyone is ready for fun and responsibility, too.

The older children are assigned to watch some of the younger ones. "Keep an eye on your brother and sister when you swim." "You make sure they have life jackets on when canoeing," etc. Some of our creative ones never leave camp. They draw and read comics. Others are into puzzles. We bring along model-building kits (with glue) and 1,000-plus piece puzzles for rainy days.

Everyone is briefed on the campsite rules.

A rough schedule is followed for sleeping and rising together. Sharing is what camping together is all about in our family. We share the sun and fresh air — also the insects and rain when it falls.

And Sometimes It Pours

Recently, we lost our new golden retriever on vacation in a tragic accident. She was run over on an isolated country back road. As a family, we worked it out.

We've all learned more about nature, each other and ourselves on every trip we've taken. We've always had fun and we're certain our kids are the biggest part of these good times. And it's an experience you don't want to miss. Try it, and take some kids along!

Hard-fought hockey competition with a lot of body checking

Good ways to see the countryside

For Kids (and Dogs) — My Wife's Checklist

- ☐ Mix of diapers
- ☐ Horseshoes
- ☐ Treats
- ☐ Baby wipes
- ☐ Bat and baseball
- ☐ Baby food
- ☐ Diaper bags
- ☐ Volleyball
- ☐ Pacifier
- ☐ Children's pain reliever
- ☐ Football
- ☐ Dog food

- ☐ Raincoats
- ☐ Frisbee
- ☐ Dog tag
- ☐ Favorite toys
- ☐ Croquet set
- ☐ Leash
- ☐ Checkers/cards
- ☐ Lots of extra clothes
- ☐ Flea collar
- ☐ Comic books
- ☐ Warm jackets
- ☐ Water bowl

- ☐ Coloring books and crayons
- ☐ Comforter
- ☐ Biscuits
- ☐ Pens, pencils and paper
- ☐ Favorite games
- ☐ Dog toy
- ☐ *And...*

Do I Bring The Pets?

If possible take him/her along. Your dog may feel more secure being with you. Remember, dogs can't read and will not know all the campground rules. It will take teamwork. And keep in mind one other thing — dogs are not allowed in national parks, and some campgrounds do not allow dogs even though they are well behaved and kept on a leash. Another thing to remember is a

name and address tag, just in case your dog gets lost in the wilderness.

Test The Waters First

Full-facility campsites with swimming and organized activities might be a good way to break-in the family on outdoor life. Most teenagers and smaller children will want to stay active. If you leave the TV and VCR at home, you will have spare time and a gap to fill. If you bring friends and the whole family, you will want to have at least a weekend to unwind and get into a new routine of

outdoor living. Some suggestions are gameboards (magnetic for wind resistance) and charades for young adults. Cards will be the answer for couples who enjoy refreshments, chips, pretzels and competition under generated lights.

Our evening hours are reserved for relaxing, reflection and togetherness. We encourage our youngsters to discover star gazing and the splendor of our universe.

Our evening ritual is a nightcap at the family campfire while recapping the day's experiences. We find this the perfect way to wind down and prepare for a good night's rest.

Visit Self-Serve Fruit Farms

There are many countryside orchards with apple, cherry, pear and plum trees where customers can choose and pick baskets of fruit. It's a wonderful experience for campers of all ages to harvest and sample the juicy freshness of just-picked fruit. And there is no better way to buy. Strawberries and blueberries can also be picked at considerable savings when in season.

Edible wild items can be found almost everywhere in North America's wooded areas. Depending on the season — raspberries, thimbleberries, and blackberries are a natural treat. A handy guide to read is Euall Gibbons *A Wild Way To Eat* which is available in most libraries.

Fun Ideas For Young and Old Kids

Try a treasure hunt. All ages will enjoy using a compass to find a hidden or buried reward. You make up the directions, distance and mark where the treasures are buried. The real benefit is acquiring survival skills, such as using and reading a compass accurately.

Another fun game is a plastic egg hunt. Place quarters in the plastic eggs and hide them. Our children are quite good at locating them (see photo). And I admit the quarters are used later for video games where available.

Nature's Music

The season of song begins in May for 8,500 or more species of birds. The stars of these spring concerts are usually males who love to croon. Their performances are for love and the purpose of establishing territorial rights. Young birds are taught and encouraged to practice their craft until they master the finer points of serenading the woods. The most popular entertainers are the meadowlark and hermit thrush. Robins also get an early start on music and provide year-round early morning natural get-up calls. It's not unusual to start whistling some of these bird songs after a few seasons of listening to music in the back-country. It's very catchy.

Tools For Quick Reference
- *Audubon Society Field Guide Series*
- *Peterson Field Guide Series*

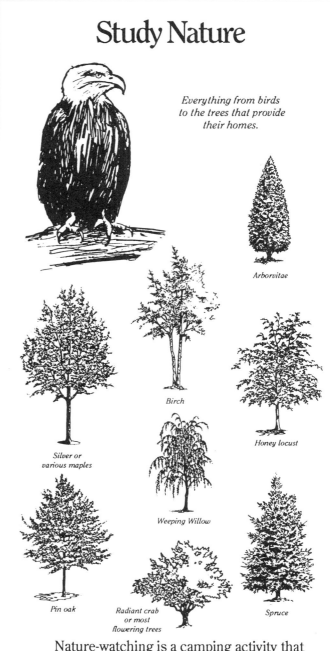

Study Nature

Everything from birds to the trees that provide their homes.

Arborvitae

Birch

Honey locust

Silver or various maples

Weeping Willow

Pin oak

Radiant crab or most flowering trees

Spruce

Nature-watching is a camping activity that has been around for generations. Binoculars should be part of this endeavor. A good selection for field binoculars is Leica's patented multirange focusing system.

Start an Outdoor Hobby

Collecting rocks, pine cones, various leaves and mounting them later can be another fun-filled activity lasting longer than the trip. The study of nature should be encouraged to run wild at the campsite.

And Record It

A good camera is the best way to record nature. Permanently capturing nature's wonders in action and building a nature album is a hobby in itself. Sometimes you only have seconds to shoot a great photograph. We recommend a 35 mm or $2^1/4$ camera, particularly an automatic that does all the work for you. Action shots become natural when you don't have to worry about light meters and setting exposures, etc. Recording the high points of your survival camp out will be for posterity. You'll appreciate the photo albums you fill.

Outdoor Subjects

Some "models" are more co-operative than others. When around cows, always keep in mind that, a bull may be near.

Outdoor Sketching A Creative Workout

All it takes is a pad, some pencils or pens and you are ready for sketching your impressions of nature. Try any subject. Start with stationary objects like trees or flowers. When you are ready to try movement, you may want a camera to capture additional reference. All of my pastel and oil paintings have been started with sketches that became permanent paintings. Anyone can improve their drawing skills with quick sketching.

Catch Up on the Classics

Remember the best-selling book you planned on reading someday? Well, here's the perfect opportunity to do it. Take it out from the library and bring it along. In fact, take several classics along for the rest of the family. You'll find good literature is contagious. Good conversations seem to flow out of books read together. We always set aside time to read and relax on our camping trips.

A Family Siesta

A nonactivity for a few hours might be the best activity for refreshing yourself and others on a hot, or humid day. Try taking a break at high noon. In southern Europe and South America, when the sun is high, workers take a long lunch and a nap. No outdoor work gets done between noon and 3:00. If you like to extend your day, rise early with nature, take an afternoon siesta and be wide awake for the cool campfire at night. It really works wonders on depressing rainy days, too.

63

PART VII

Setting up the Campsite

Author on bivouac

Selecting the Campsite

When you set up a natural campsite, here are some things to remember. Do it always at least two hours before sunset. The terrain should be checked out for dead trees and limbs. They can be extremely dangerous in high winds. In isolated areas, be aware of sites below the high-water mark. Flash floods can cause total wipeouts. Water availability is important at all times. Sources of fuel may be critical in the winter.

Family or Group Tents

An eight to ten person tent can be set up in minutes when you are familiar with the setup and takedown procedures.

These modern tents have screened window areas and are enclosed on the bottom to prevent seepage. You can rig lights for indoor activities. They fold easily into a compact storage bag for transporting.

Quick Tent Setups

Self-pitching tents are the latest way to setup a shelter without assembly. A dome-shaped tent can be erected effortlessly without pounding stakes. In a free standing tent the frame is outside — meaning more room on the inside. You can also select a light-weight tunnel type which is staked and resists high winds. We recommend a tent that allows you to sit up and is easier to move around in.

Free-standing tent

Basic Tents

If you like it a little rougher, consider military poncho tents that snap together. Just a few ropes and stakes, and you are in business. A good idea is to tie your rope ends to trees approximately ten feet apart. An A-frame always shores the middle up. See illustration for strengthening a basic tent. Don't forget to dig an eight-inch deep trench around the sides to prevent water seepage. Also use a plastic ground cloth inside the tent. The old standby camping tent for larger parties is the A-frame type. Many old-time campers still appreciate its basic design and durability.

Tent Selection Checklist

- ☐ Four-season type (winter use, too)
- ☐ Sleeping capacity (at least three)
- ☐ Weight (lighter for backpacking)
- ☐ Fabrics (waterproof nylon)
- ☐ Zippers (plastic-cord model)
- ☐ Poles (aluminum)
- ☐ Floors (thicker material)

Accessories: Seam sealer (use on sewing holes)

Build Your Own Shelter

From nature, an angled windbreaker shelter can be fashioned from your surroundings. All that is necessary is a sturdy tree to build onto. Just extend a support pole across the tree support and a pole support, then tie these elements together. Angle six to eight sticks across the support pole. Cover with poncho or tarp (see illustration). Be sure the backside is placed into the wind. Leaves, grass or pine needles can be substituted for an air mattress. You can also build a fire reflector wall by stacking green logs on the exposed side. This will reflect your fire's warmth.

Natural shelter for poncho or tarp

Firewall

Utilize trees — A-frame storm support

Rain trench

65

Knots — Tying One Is Easy

Just like in the old scout training manual, you should know how to tie and keep things securely together in the field. We recommend the double half-hitch to fasten a rope to a tree, post, pole or branch. Use a sheet bend knot to join two ropes, cords or straps together. Another popular knot with many uses is the bowline knot. Its single loop will not become smaller because of tension, and it's a great way to keep animals securely tied up. See the illustrations for directions.

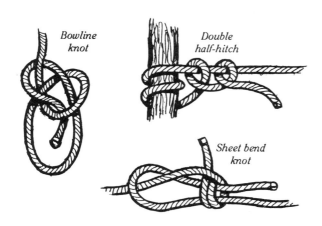

Bowline knot

Double half-hitch

Sheet bend knot

Campsite Lighting

A propane lantern that is adjustable from a bright 175 candlepower to dim night light is an ideal choice for all-around outside lighting. Expect a propane model to burn about 15 hours on a 16.4 -ounce cylinder. Inside the tent, our choice is a 6-volt battery powered lamp with soft, diffused lighting. (Only use battery operated lights inside a tent.)

Propane lantern

Wilderness Knives

The jack of all trades is the popular Swiss army knife. It can include a large blade, can opener, screwdriver, bottle openers, universal wrench, nail file, compass and map ruler, fish scaler, scissors, corkscrew, tweezer and more. Everyone should have one. We still recommend a sturdy stockman knife (multibladed) for tough jobs. The

Multipurpose Swiss army knife

three-inch long blade that folds should be made of high-carbon, cutlery-style tempered steel. It's a good back-up knife.

Stockman-type knife

Survival Saw

Space-saving folding saws are the way to go if they feature strong rigidity with a full stroke. There's a whole new generation of saws to choose from. Pick one that has 20 inches of rigid blade action and folds down for easy storage. A good mate is the double-duty hammer/hatchet or steel shaft camp axe for chopping firewood.

66

Chopping Wood Safely

Everyone knows someone who has had a close call chopping wood. There are ways to reduce the risk of injury, however. Do not swing a hatchet; use it only as a wedge. Use another piece of wood to drive in the hatchet after starting it as a wedge. Saw wood to one-foot lengths for easy handling. And keep the wood you're splitting at waist level. Use all-steel hatchets. Be sure to wear work gloves to avoid splinters and always split kindling from the grain end.

NOTE:

Safety goggles and work gloves recommended

Use steel shaft camp axe as wedge

How to Start a Fire Without Kindling Wood

Many years ago I was a newspaper delivery boy and folded thousands of papers weekly. When someone requests a fire, I start folding. It's great tinder when the winds are light and it's a good way to get rid of old newspapers that can't be recycled.

"Folded logs"

How to Build a Tepee Fire

Gather dry, dead branches and break the into kindling. Pile them in the middle. Set up larger pieces of dry wood in the shape of a tepee. Fallen branches and dead tree trunks are excellent fuel sources. Light your fire away from the upwind side. Check out the campground regulations to see if permits are required for open fires. Some parks (especially during dry spells) allow only charcoal cooking fires in shielded cookers. Make sure fires are always out before you leave your campsite

Tepee fire

Extra Blankets

A set of wool blankets is a handy thing to have around. If your sleeping bag gets wet, blankets can be folded into a bed that offers some woolen warmth. They also are a good way to stay warm till your tepee fire gets going — a good defense against hypothermia.

Makeshift blanket bag

Unwelcome Campsite Visitors

Insect repellent should be freely used, especially to ward off ticks. Ticks are small insects approximately one-eighth inch in length. When attached to the skin, they expand five to seven times their original size.

The best treatment for Lyme disease, which ticks carry, is prevention:

- Wear shoes and socks always when hiking or backpacking.
- Wear a long-sleeved shirt.
- Check regularly for ticks.
- Comb or brush hair after hiking.
- Keep clothes, towels, etc., off the ground.
- Use spray/powders on pets.
- Use formulated tick-protection insect repellent.

Ticks expand five to seven times original size

67

Best Way to Fool Bears

Don't use the nearby tree to hang your food on. Bears can see, smell and learn. The last campers at your site probably taught them where to look for food. Hide your food in heavy-lined plastic bags in an area away from the campsite. Bears lose interest fast when the "cupboard is bare." Also promptly clean up and get rid of any garbage.

WARNING: Do Not Feed Wild Animals

No matter how friendly wildlife may seem, the best way to avoid misunderstandings and hospital bills is not to feed, invite or touch any wild animal. That includes bears, squirrels, rabbits, deer, wolves, wildcats, birds and other creatures that potentially carry various diseases. Dispose of garbage that might attract hungry or curious wildlife.

Reasons Not to Feed Wild Animals

Besides deaths attributed to both Grizzly and Black bears, there are infectious diseases to contend with. Talaremia, commonly known as rabbit fever, is an infectious disease that can be transmitted to humans through physical contact.

Every year there are hundreds of raccoons found with rabies. Your pet animal, if not inoculated against the disease, can contact it and pass it along to humans.

Skunks are confirmed to carry rabies in the western and midwest regions in significant numbers. Our advice: Do not feed or handle wild animals.

PART VIII

Exploring the Backcountry

Backpacking and Hiking

Try to stay under 25 pounds of total weight for a weekend jaunt. We recommend an alloy rigid frame backpack that is lightweight. Load it up and road-test it before buying. Expect to spend at least a hundred dollars for a good one. It's worth it. Make sure your clothing is right for weather changes and drops in temperature. Rain gear is essential. Make sure you carry a canteen of fresh water. And pack a ministove for boiling water. Measuring approximately three-inches high by three-inches in diameter, it fits easily in a backpack. A great way to exercise is hiking. Keep in mind walking at a brisk pace (3 mph) burns off 200-250 calories in an hour, and 3,500 calories burned converts to one pound lost. Not bad.

Know Your Limits

Too stiff a pace can bring on exhaustion before you reach your destination or the end of the trip. On the trail, check out your progress and take a breather. Fatigue can make you careless. Accidents often happen when the body is tired. Resist pushing yourself or others past their comfort level. You are vacationing, not training for a marathon. Get rest and allow for difficult terrain, weather changes and the unexpected. Take along some energy boosters — raisins, granola bars, mixed nuts and fruit snacks for a quick picker-upper. And it's a good idea when traveling alone to tell someone where you are going and when you expect to return.

Backpack Gear Checklist

Pack at top (keep light)
- [ ] Clothing (extra warm)
- [ ] Rain gear/long johns
- [ ] Dried food/water
- [ ] Plastic bags/matches

Pockets at top (keep light)
- [ ] Map/minibinoculars
- [ ] Compass/signal mirror
- [ ] Canteen with cup
- [ ] Swiss army knife
- [ ] Sunglasses/sunscreen
- [ ] Repellent/chlorine or iodine tablets
- [ ] Personals/toilet articles

Pack at middle (keep light to medium)
- [ ] Tent/poles/pegs
- [ ] Portable burner (butane)
- [ ] Pots/pans/utensils
- [ ] 2-quart thermos (hot soup)
- [ ] Flashlight/batteries
- [ ] Hygiene supplies
- [ ] Fishing gear/nylon cord
- [ ] Change of clothing
- [ ] Blanket/ground liner

Pack at bottom (keep heaviest)
- [ ] Sleeping bag
- [ ] Air mattress
- [ ] Saw/hatchet

- [ ] Cleaning supplies
- [ ] First aid kit (also snake bite kit)
- [ ] Sketching materials/camera
- [ ] *An Illustrated Handbook for Surviving Family Camp Outs*

Pockets at bottom (keep heaviest)
- [ ] Snacks
- [ ] Mittens
- [ ] Extra socks
- [ ] Flare

Backpack

Top-loading with double compartment flexible frame

Proper use of handle bars

sure stopping power. Another feature to include is a quick release for saddle vertical adjustments. A map, compass and odometer are a must for off-the-road bicycling (see Bicycling Gear Checklist).

Bicycling Tips

Start slowly for the first few miles, especially in cold weather, pedaling in low gears. Proper use of handlebars will help you avoid aches and pains. (See illustration). Wear a helmet: it's mandatory and a lifesaver over rugged terrain. Biking gloves are a good idea to protect hands in a fall. For comfort, lightweight jackets and easy-to-move bike shorts are best. Be sure they are chamois-padded in the seat bottoms. Your shoes should be especially designed for cycling. Stiff-shafted athletic shoes are best for riding support and firm peddling. Your hiking companions should include a water bottle for refreshment and a bike pump for slow leaks. For safety, include a reflective safety vest, bike reflectors, headlamp and a rear mirror.

Bicycling — Main and Back Roads

Map out your trip On a topographical map check for contour and elevation lines. This will help you avoid hilly country if possible. The weather is always a factor to consider. Strong winds and extreme heat should be weighed against the distance you plan on covering in a day. You might want to plan a restaurant or historic home stop in your days activities.

You should also be knowledgeable of the traffic on roadways. Children with only off-the-road biking experience should not try busy roads. Trucks can be dangerous with wind-blast effects. Avoid heavily traveled roads.

Back-roads bicycling Off-the-road biking is in the same family as cross-country skiing. Movement is what it is all about. A mountain bike is designed and constructed for these moves. Their drive-train components handle stress situations with ease. These fat-tired bikes can manage rough roads and the handlebars are made for out-of-the-saddle climbing. Make sure the bike brakes are of cantilever design for

untain bike

Bicycling Gear Checklist
- [ ] Helmet
- [ ] Cycling shoes and shorts
- [ ] Gloves and shoe covers
- [ ] Rain gear/garbage bags (utilize as covers)
- [ ] Reflective safety vest
- [ ] Repair kit and pump
- [ ] 2-quart thermos/water bottle
- [ ] Tools (knife, flashlight, etc.)
- [ ] Basic safety equipment (mirror, headlamp, reflectors)
- [ ] First aid kit
- [ ] Personals

Canoe Camping

Utilizing streams and rivers with a canoe is the easiest way to probe deep into the wilderness. Canoes are very maneuverable and, when handled properly, are very stable in the water (do not stand up in a canoe). A good no-maintenance choice is one made of aluminum. Start with a 15-footer. There's plenty of room for you and provisions for extended journeys. You should secure these supplies if you expect rough water. No canoe or inflatable craft should be without life jackets. Always team up. And don't forget to bring the knee pads.

Selecting the Right Canoe

The craft you choose to paddle should be suited to your water skills. Kneeling and using a single-bladed paddle in a 15-foot solo canoe requires riding in water with little back-up. Open canoeing in turbulent water takes a lot of strength and expertise.

We recommend the tandem open canoe as the best way to start your canoeing career. Teamwork is what it's all about. Always put the beginner in the bow. The stern paddler is responsible for the placement of the canoe. Always pack an open canoe with low and even distribution of weight (heaviest items at the bottom). It's important to be knowledgeable of the recommended weight displacement figures. The design and size determines this. Keep items you're using constantly in easy-to-reach areas.

How About Rafts?

Riding rafts is pure fun. Very little experience is necessary — you visually bounce off the rocks and sometimes think you're on a bumper boat.

There's plenty of room for a family and gear on paddle or oar rafts. We recommend a paddle type if everyone wants to get into the act. Outboard (under 3hp) can be of great assistance when traveling upstream.

Our last choice of water running is tubing. We feel it's basically unsafe even with a life jacket. It should be avoided.

Survival tip: On unfamiliar streams with rapids, check them out by walking along the bank before road testing them in a canoe or craft.

One personal floating device per person

Canoeing Gear Checklist

- ☐ PFD (personal flotation device) for each person
- ☐ Extra paddles
- ☐ Knee pads
- ☐ Lines for securing supplies
- ☐ Outboard motor — under 3 hp (optional)
- ☐ Signal lights (SOS)
- ☐ Storm gear/extra clothes
- ☐ Water/food/snacks
- ☐ Bailing pails and extra flotation devices
- ☐ Tools (knife, flashlight, etc.)
- ☐ Topo maps/map magnifier lamp
- ☐ First aid kit
- ☐ Personals

Cross-Country Skiing

This is a kick and glide exercise designed to help you sleep well especially after a full day of ski touring. Be sure to get in shape before you try this old Scandinavian means of recreational travel in the winter. It's best when the snow is fresh and the trails are clear. Layers of clothes are a good idea for cross-country skiing.

Snowmobiling

It's similar to driving except that you have a lot less protection from the elements. Special clothing is absolutely necessary. Insulated suits and felt-lined boots are recommended. Sleds loaded with camping gear can be towed (check snowmobile manufacturer recommendations). Frozen lakes and rivers are smooth and easy for snowmobiling, but always make sure they are frozen solid.

Survival tips: It's a lot more fun if you're joined by another snowmobiler and it's safer too. An on-the-road emergency kit should include tools, oil, gas (where legal to carry), extra-thick sandwiches and a thermos of warm coffee or cocoa.

The Ol' Swimming Hole

Experienced swimmers can tell you that no body of water is ever the same. Drop-offs, undercurrents and pollution must be considered. Never swim alone. Life jackets are absolutely necessary for all water sports. Swimming in the pool in your backyard can be dangerous if you eat and then swim. For children, consider only the areas marked as safe, shallow, and gradual drop-off. Lifeguards or an excellent swimmer should be present. (For swimming emergencies, see mouth-to-mouth resuscitation steps for drowning victims in Part XIII — Life-Threatening Emergencies).

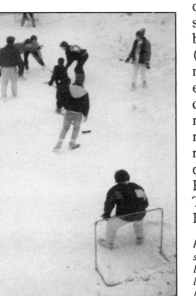

Family hockey games sometimes get a little rough. But everyone is required to line up and shake hands at the end of the game.

73

Reading Nature

Nature, both day and night, helps you find the right directions. During the day, the sun rises in the east and sets in the west. To find directions at any time during the day, simply push a stick in the ground. Mark the top of the stick's east shadow. As the shadow advances approximately two inches, make another mark. This represents 10 to 15 minutes. Now draw a line through your first mark and second mark, extending it a foot beyond. Place your left foot on the first mark and the other foot on the end of the drawn line.

If you are in the northern temperature zone, you are facing directly north. If you are in the southern temperature zone, you are facing directly south.

At night, find the North Star and walk towards it to go north. The illustration on the next page shows how to visually find its position between the Big Dipper and Little Dipper.

Visually draw a straight line between the two stars at the end of the Big Dipper. It will point to the North Star. It works, but we still strongly recommend maps and a compass to detail your directions whenever traveling in the wilderness.

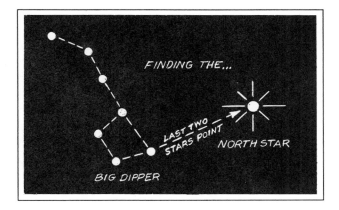

How to Select and Use a Compass

For the backcountry, when using a map, the best choice is an orienting compass that computes accurate directions and scale distances. Just turn a dial. Otherwise, you must become a navigator utilizing declination and figuring the angular difference of the true north and magnetic north. You must have a map to provide the proper directions when trails twist and turn. Compasses without a map backup can only point the directions in a straight line. Map it out — measure directions and use a protractor-type compass for accuracy.

How to Read a Topographic Map

You can actually read between the lines with these maps. Lines that are contoured closer indicate elevation steepness. Lines spaced further apart represent a gradual elevation change. River and stream flow are in the pointed direction lines. These points indicate upstream flow. Topographic maps are available from the U.S. Geologic Survey (see outdoor reference section).

Automatic adjustable declination compass

To Predict the Weather — Just Keep Your Eyes on the Clouds

Oncoming storm clouds are usually the result of cumulus clouds that become larger and push higher in the atmosphere as the day advances.

Winds blowing steadily from the north in cold climates can foretell a blizzard on the way. These high cloud types are called cirrus clouds, and they can multiply and come with strong winds.

Rain generally comes with stratus type clouds. Good signs are cirrus and cirrostratus clouds.

When the wind velocity rises, a change in weather is usually imminent. Stay alert and listen to weather reports when possible from the U.S. Weather Bureau. Be prepared with a good rain suit (two-ply sanforized denim cotton always works) and a beaked cap to keep raindrops out of your eyes or glasses. Don't forget to waterproof your shoes.

Tip: To create a makeshift for an emergency rain poncho, cut arms and neck holes in a plastic trash bag and wear as a cape.

Interpreting Contour Lines

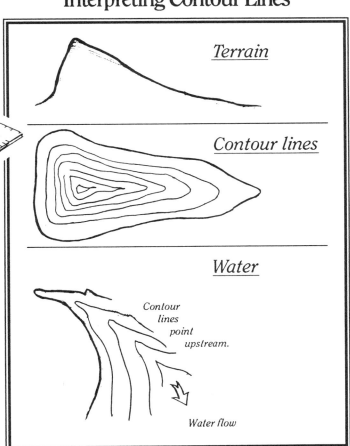

Four Main Classes of Clouds

Type	Prediction	How to Recognize
Cirrus clouds	Fair weather	High clouds that resemble thin streaks or curls usually four miles or more high.
Cumulus clouds	Potential rain maker	Fluffy, white, with vertical development.
Cumulonimbus clouds (not Illustrated)	Thunderstorms	They pile up into huge formations.
Stratus clouds	Generally means rain or snow	Low gray clouds spreading an even gray layer over the sky.
Altostratus clouds	Weather on hold	Middle clouds spreading and veiling sun or moon. Usually two – four miles high.

NOTE: *More than one hundred different kinds of clouds are distinguishable to the trained eye. See illustrations.*

Other Weather Signs

Rapidly shifting winds mean an unsettled atmosphere and a likely change in the weather. Trees show the undersides of the leaves when the wind shifts from the usual direction. Silver maple leaves are easy to spot as their bottoms are silver. Smoke that flattens out indicates stormy weather. Perched birds always face into the wind and when birds and insects fly low to the ground due to heavy moisture-laden air, figure rain's on the way. Mosquito activity increases before a storm. One good sign: Bee activity increases before fair weather.

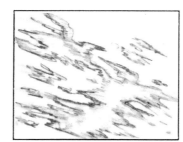

Cirrus clouds

Stratus clouds

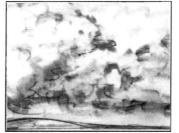

Cumulus clouds

Altostratus clouds

76

PART X

Some Things to Watch Out For

Poison Ivy and Their Family Friends

Skin contact with the oil found in the ubiquitous ivy, poison oak and poison sumac results in painful, itchy and blistering rashes. Just brushing against these plants or standing in the smoke of burning poison ivy leaves can ruin your camp out and more. Wear protective clothing, especially on arms and legs when in any wooded area. If your skin contacts one of these plants, shower as soon as possible and wash your clothes. In severe cases, cortisone treatment may be necessary. (See illustrations below for visual identification of these plants.)

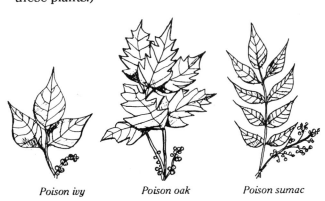

Poison ivy   *Poison oak*   *Poison sumac*

Bears, Bees and Bites (Animals and Insects)

Bears should be avoided. Troublesome animals such as black bears are considered friendly when compared to the fierce grizzly bear. Grizzlies in our national parks are exceedingly scarce. As previously stated never feed bears or any other animals.

Avoid bees, especially in a dry season when they may be attracted to your picnic table. If a bee stings, remove the stinger and clean the area surrounding the sting. Use an antiseptic to disinfect the sting area. If you are allergic, seek medical aid immediately.

Bites should be avoided. Treat any animal bite for possible infection and rabies and seek medical attention immediately. (To determine if the attacking animal is rabid it may be necessary to analyze the attacking animal. Capture it if possible). Most mosquito bites can be limited with insect repellents, screens and avoiding exposure in the hours when they are most active. Also stay away from wet or damp areas when mosquito populations are high.

Snakes, Spiders and Scorpions

Snakes

The dark side of outdoor living is contending with the possibility of highly poisonous bites. Snake bites can be fatal if the reptile is poisonous and the bite is left untreated. In North America, the poisonous snakes include the rattlesnake, cottonmouth (also known as the water moccasin), copperhead and coral snake. The rattlesnake can be found in almost any section of the country.

The illustration and chart below tell how to indentify a poisonous snake.

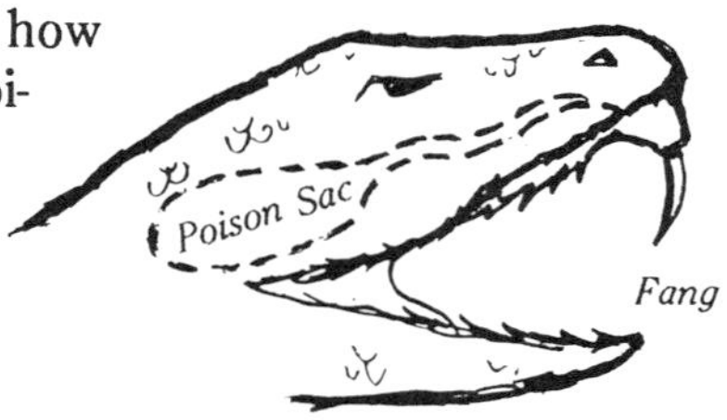

Poison Sac

Fang

Ways to Avoid Snake Bites

Wear boots and heavy trousers. Watch where you walk. Most bites happen when you accidentally step on a snake. A walking stick is a good weapon if an area has an abundance of snakes. Do not place your hands in a hole, in bushes, under rocks or river banks. Probe with a stick before you touch.

If bitten, check the punctures. One or two fang punctures at the site of the bite (sometimes three or four) generally indicate a poisonous snake. Even if you have a snake bite kit, you could be allergic to the antivenin. Remain calm and seek medical assistance at once. If possible, try to kill the snake without deforming it's head. Make sure it's dead before handling. Take it along to the medical facility for identification purposes.

Poisonous Snake Identification Chart for USA

Name	Characteristics	Primary Location	Group	Venom Type
Coral	Black nose Rounded eyes Red, yellow and black rings	Southeast	Fixed fangs	Neurotoxic dominant
Rattlesnake (27 species)	Tri-shaped head Slitted eyes Set of rattles at end of tail*	All over country	Folded fangs	Hemotoxic dominant or neurotoxic dominant
Cottonmouth (Water moccasin)	Tri-shaped head Slitted eyes White coloring inside mouth	Southeast and south central	Folded fangs	Hemotoxic dominant
Copperhead	Tri-shaped head Slitted eyes	Southeast and south central	Folded fangs	Hemotoxic dominant

*NOTE: *Rattlesnakes may strike first and rattle afterwards.*

78

Spiders

Bites are more serious for the elderly or very young children. The black widow spider and brown recluse spider can be identified from the illustrations below.

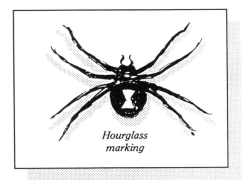

Black widows feature an hourglass marking on their underside.

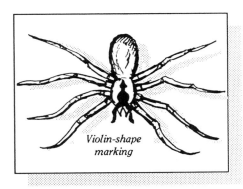

The brown recluse is characterized by a dark violin-shaped marking (top front).

Immediate medical attention is required (with the dead spider for identification).

Tarantula spiders are not usually as serious as those described above.

Scorpions

Some species are more poisonous than others, but all have stings that are very harmful to young children. The scorpion resembles a small lobster. It stings from the tail which arches over its back. The victim should remain calm, watch for signs of shock and seek medical attention, preferably at the nearest hospital emergency room.

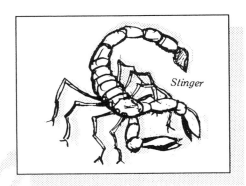

PART XI

The Nitty-Gritty

Stay Clean — Personal Hygiene is Important

Your hands especially should be kept clean to avoid spreading germs. Take special care when handling food. Keep hot water in your thermos for quick cleanups. It's also a good idea to have hot water overnight to wash or shave with in the morning. A three-inch-diameter backpack stove is ideal for warming up water.

Today's parks and facilities can provide daily showers with hot water. Modern camper vehicles can also provide a quick shower. For backpackers, an outdoor shower tip: Fill an ordinary trash bag with water, hang it from a tree limb and let the water warm in the sun. Puncture the bottom of the bag and you now have a perfect and refreshing shower.

*Three-inch
backpack-size stove*

Or take an air bath. Remove as much of your clothing as practical while exposing your skin to the air and sunlight for a short time. When soap is unavailable, sand or even ashes can even be substituted.

When There Is No Outhouse or Facility

Military procedure is to dig far away from where you eat and live. They call it a slit trench. It's narrow and deep — so it can be straddled. A shovel, a pile of dirt and paper is kept near. When your "duty" is done, shovel dirt in the trench or hole over the contents. Use the trench until it fills to a foot from ground level, then fill it with 12 inches of top soil and mark the area. Next, move to a new area. This may sound primitive, but it is the only way in isolated backwoods areas to keep your constitution intact and avoid contamination.

When Special Medication is Required

Campers suffering from diabetes, glaucoma, epilepsy, hemophilia and reaction to certain medications (such as penicillin) or to insect stings should wear a bracelet or necklace listing blood type, allergy or serious condition. An alternative is to carry a card with the same information.

Keeping Water on Tap

Bring it along or get your drinking water only from known and approved sources.

For water obtained from lakes or rivers, here are some tips. Go upstream and far out and deep if you have the means. Forget backwaters and stagnated areas. Look for incoming streams. But always boil the water for a minimum of four to five minutes; 15 minutes is safer. Treat the water with chlorine or iodine tablets. Portable filters can be used, but keep in mind they take time and some do not handle guardia lamblia — a tough protozoan that's hard to kill. We definitely recommend you substitute with other liquids such as juice, skim milk, soda, and ration drinking water for tea, coffee and mouth rinse until you reach a safe source for replenishment.

When fresh water is not available, here's our
SURVIVAL WATER CHART

Source	Methods for obtaining water and making potable	Water purification techniques
Streams, rivers & lakes	Always go up stream. Avoid stagnant areas and industrial pollution. If possible, obtain water over 100 feet from shoreline. Look for deep waters.	Best way Boil for 30 minutes. For high altitudes and suspect areas, boil for over an hour. Other treatments: chemicals Use either iodine or chlorine tablets (available from most pharmacies) to purify. Iodine is more effective against protozoans. Filtration systems Pump-operated models require time to process. Can filter down to 0.01 microns.
Rain	Catch water in clean pails, containers and tarps.	
Beach	Dig deep holes allowing water to seep in. Build a hot wood fire and heat large rocks. Drop them in the fire to create steam. Hold a clean cloth over the steam. Wring absorbed water over pot.	
Desert	Wherever you find damp surface sand, dig a deep hole allowing water to seep in.	

NOTE: *Survival water must be purified. Boiling is always recommended.*

Avoid Too Much Sun

Sun damage is cumulative and if you're fair skinned, have blond or red hair with blue eyes, you should avoid excessive sun exposure. If your hair is thin, be sure to wear a hat of some sort. The sun's maximum potential for skin damage is between 11 a.m. and 3 p.m. Sun blocks are helpful, but protective clothing that is thick and woven tightly prevents harmful radiation from penetrating. A bad burn should be treated with cool compresses, calamine lotion or over-the-counter antihistamines for relief of itching. If severe symptoms develop, it is critical that you get medical attention. Tan may be "in", but it is wiser to avoid the after effects of long-term excessive sun exposure.

Take Care of Your Feet

Boots are your best bet for the outdoors, but a comfortable fit is everything. Always buy the lightest boot you can find at an outdoor equipment specialty store. Full or top grain leather is my choice. Ankle support is a must with padding at the collar. Break them in before the trip. Another tip is to double up on your socks. The inside pair should be thin cotton and the outside pair a thick wool. This combination handles perspiration and allows slow evaporation. Always have extra dry socks for backup. Keep a foot care kit handy, too.

HD hiking boots

Drink Plenty of Liquids

The average adult loses up to three quarts of water daily. This water must be replaced. To prevent dehydration when using a lot of energy, drink small amounts of fluids regularly. Your urine will keep you posted on becoming dehydrated. A dark color can suggest you should be drinking more water.

PART XII

First Aid Treatment and Checklist

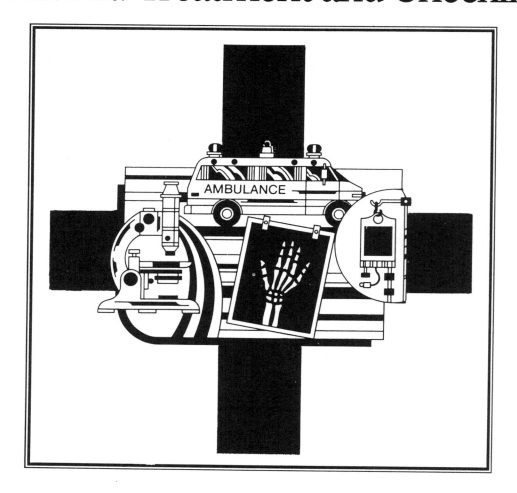

Muscle Aches and Pains

Over-exercising and fatigue or even keeping a limb in one position for a prolonged period can cause a muscle cramp. These cramps often occur in your foot, calf or thigh, especially in the middle of the night. Massaging stimulates local circulation and this helps to relax the affected muscle.

If the cramp is in the foot, turn your toes up toward your thigh and bend the foot back. For cramps in your calf, stand up and place most or your weight on the unaffected leg and massage the cramp.

For thigh cramps, lie down and massage the cramp area. Rest and heat often are helpful. Any pain that is severe or prolonged needs medical attention.

Strains and Sprains

Apply an ice pack on and off for the first 24 hours to relieve swelling. Follow with warm compresses to increase blood flow and stimulate healing in the afflicted area. Get medical attention if pain, swelling or discoloration continues. Cold compresses can be fashioned from frozen food pouches if you have a camper freezer.

Cold compress

84

Foot Blisters

Wash with soap and water. Do not remove skin over the blister when it breaks. Protect the area with a bandage until the new skin tissue is ready. Be sure to check the instructions in your foot care kit for additional treatment.

Toothache

Try sucking on an ice cube or massaging with ice on the aching tooth. Intense cold often is almost as effective as novocain. Applying heat may spread an infection if the pain is the result of an abcessed tooth. Get dental assistance as soon as possible.

Backache — Exercise and Treatment

Lie on your back with knees bent and feet flat on the ground. Use both hands to wrap around your knee — slowly. Pull that knee up to your chest. Repeat ten times with each leg. Applying heat to the affected area will help in most cases.

Heat Exhaustion

High temperatures and humidity with prolonged exposure can result in heat exhaustion. Get in the shade or a cooler area. Lie down. Loosen clothing. Place cool, wet cloths on the forehead and body. If you have a fan, use it. Seek medical attention promptly if the condition worsens.

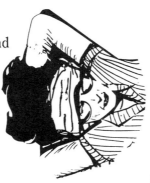

Hypothermia

When the body temperature drops below 95 degrees, chilling occurs. Remove wet or damp clothes. Get out of the wind. Warm your body with a campfire and a sleeping bag. Use additional blankets if available. Drink hot liquids. Keep warm and rest. Seek medical attention as soon as possible.

Frostbite

Toes, fingers, nose and ears are the most often affected parts of the body that freeze when exposed to very low temperatures. As frostbite develops, the skin becomes white or greyish yellow. Blisters may form in later stages. For immediate treatment, gently wrap the frostbitten area in warm materials. Place the victim's frostbitten part in warm (not hot) water 100 – 104 degrees. Test the water with a thermometer or dip your forearm to check its heat. Do not break blisters. Stop the warming process when feeling begins to come back. Seek medical attention promptly and try to keep frostbitten parts elevated in the meantime. In severe frostbite cases, cover the areas with warm materials and rush the victim to the nearest hospital emergency room. Dressing warmly and staying dry is an absolute must for winter campers.

Cuts and Puncture Wounds

Always use direct pressure to control bleeding or severe cuts. Make sure your hands are clean before touching any wound. When bleeding has stopped, wash the wound with soap and water. Cover the wound with a sterile dressing. Beyond this point a doctor should advise. Seek medical attention if bleeding does not stop, the wound is severe, there are signs of infection, or you have doubts of tetanus immunization, especially if it is a deep puncture wound.

Get a Tetanus Booster

If you haven't had a tetanus booster in ten years, get one before you camp. Once you have been infected, medical techniques against tetanus are only marginally effective. In event of a wound or puncture, get a booster shot immediately if it's been at least five years since your last one. Tetanus boosters are needed every ten years for resisting infection by the tetanus organism.

First Aid and Medical Emergency Kit Checklist

- ☐ 4 x 4 sterile gauze pads — nonstick
- ☐ 3-inch-wide wide roll of gauze bandage
- ☐ 3-inch elastic bandage (ideal for wrapping sprains)
- ☐ 1-inch size roll of adhesive tape
- ☐ Butterfly bandages
- ☐ Adhesive strips
- ☐ Cotton-tipped swabs
- ☐ Absorbent cotton roll
- ☐ Hydrogen peroxide 3% solution
- ☐ Soap bar
- ☐ Calamine lotion
- ☐ Acetaminophen (for children under 16)
- ☐ Aspirin — regular strength (check warnings for usage on label)
- ☐ Antihistamine for allergic reactions (tablet form)
- ☐ Foot care kit
- ☐ Snake bite kit
- ☐ Scissors, tweezers, safety pins
- ☐ Thermometer (oral)
- ☐ Blankets for warmth
- ☐ Scarf for sling
- ☐ Fan for heatstroke

First Aid K I T
SURVIVING Family camp outs

PART XIII

Life-Threatening Emergencies

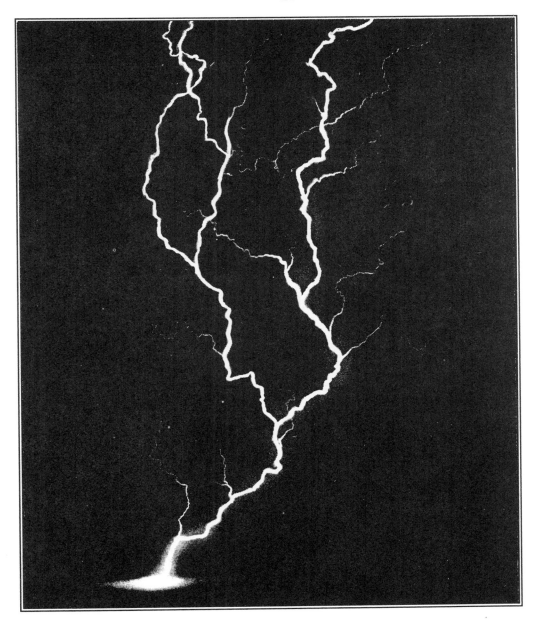

Accidents do happen and how you react in an isolated area is sometimes important to your survival. Just taking the top off a soup can sometimes leads to an unexpected nasty cut. You should know how to stop bleeding with a pressure bandage. Cleaning and dressing is important for avoiding infections before professional medical treatment can be administered. In any emergency stay calm and seek medical assistance as soon as possible. Substitution tip: Emergency dressings can be fashioned out of sanitary napkins. Cut to the right size.

Direct Pressure for Bleeding

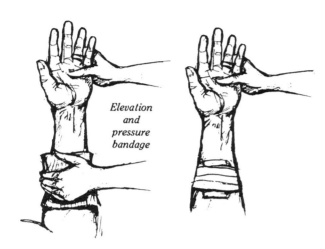

Elevation and pressure bandage

Place a thick sterile or clean compress directly over the entire wound and press firmly with the palm of your hand. If the wound is bleeding severely, elevate the limb above the victim's heart and continue direct pressure.

Once bleeding stops or slows, apply a pressure bandage to hold the compress in place. Place the center of the bandage directly over the compress. Pull steadily while wrapping both ends around the injury. Tie a knot over the compress. Do not tie so tightly that it cuts off circulation. Keep the limb elevated until bleeding stops. Seek medical attention immediately.

Burns — First, Second and Third Degree

Put the burned area in cold water (not iced) or apply a cold water compress until pain subsides. Do not apply butter or grease to burn. Cover the burned area with a dry, nonfluffy sterile bandage. Elevate burned arms or legs, if possible. Seek medical attention immediately.

Adult Mouth-to-Mouth Resuscitation Steps

If the victim ceases breathing:
1. Be sure the victim is on a hard, flat surface. Quickly clear the mouth and airways of all foreign material.
2. Tilt the victim's head backward by placing the palm of your hand on the forehead and the fingers of your other hand under the bony part of chin.
3. Pinch the victim's nostrils with thumb and index finger. Take a deep breath. Place your mouth tightly over the victim's mouth. Give two quick breaths.
4. Stop blowing when the victim's chest is expanding. Remove your mouth from the victim's mouth and turn your head toward the victim's chest so your ear is over the mouth. Listen for air being exhaled. Watch for the victim's chest to fall. Repeat the breathing procedure. Always seek medical assistance.

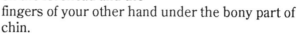

Infant Mouth-to-Mouth-and-Nose Resuscitation Steps

To breathe air into an infant's lungs: place your mouth over the infant's mouth and nose. Blow two breaths so that his or her chest rises. Do not blow air as forcefully as in an adult. Take a breath between each of your breaths. Always seek medical assistance.

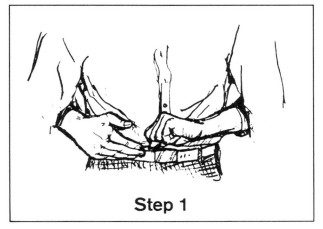

Step 1

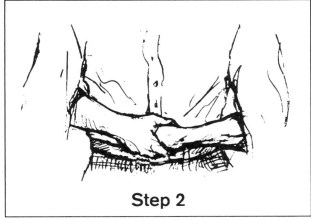

Step 2

Heimlich Maneuver for Adults Choking

1. Correct placement of fist with thumb side against victim's stomach slightly above navel and below ribs and breastbone.

2. If victim is standing or sitting, stand behind victim with your arms around the waist. Place fist as shown. Hold fist with other hand. Give four quick, forceful upward thrusts.

It may be necessary to repeat the procedure several times. Always seek medical assistance.

Heimlich Maneuver for Children Choking

Stand behind child with arms around waist.

For a child

Place thumb side of fist against child's stomach slightly above navel and below ribs and breastbone. Hold fist with other hand. Give four quick, forceful upward thrusts. It may be necessary to repeat procedure several times. Always seek medical assistance.

Heart Attacks, Strokes and Fractures (Neck and Back)

These emergencies require immediate medical assistance. They are too serious to treat and move without medical knowledge and supervision. Stay calm and get medical help as soon as possible.

How to Signal for Help...SOS

The internationally recognized signal of distress. You can use lights or flags to send an SOS – three dots, three dashes and three dots. For lights...short flashes for dots and long for dashes.

When using flags, hold them on the left side for dashes and on the right side for dots. Keep repeating the signal.

Use a mirror for signaling planes and helicopters by bouncing the sunlight directly at the air craft. Wave both arms or lay on back with your arms stretched together overhead. This signals you need medical assistance.

If isolated, use natural materials to form symbols or a message that can be seen from the air. Use rocks, brush, foliage or even snow blocks. Smoke is also another attention getter. The international distress signal is three columns of smoke.

PART XIV

Our Favorite Time and Place

Autumn in Door County, Wisconsin. It's the change of seasonal colors in the almost 80-mile-long peninsula, a panorama of beauty rivalling Cape Cod with its mixture of northern trees merging into a rustic rainbow. A constant fresh breeze spreads these brilliant leaf colors everywhere. Every year, Door County is a sight to behold and capture, at least in memory.

After Sturgeon Bay, you'll want to start on the Green Bay side (Route 42) and work your way up through quaint villages such as Egg Harbor, Fish Creek, Ephraim and Sister Bay. Plan on making unplanned stops at unique gift shops, boutiques and galleries sprinkled throughout the shore line. For the style-conscious traveler, there are sports and clothing stores, too. Be sure to visit the Door Peninsula Winery in Carlsville (approximately nine miles north of Sturgeon Bay). While being treated to a guided tour, you'll enjoy wine, jam and cheese tasting.

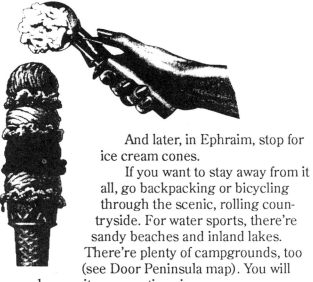

And later, in Ephraim, stop for ice cream cones.

If you want to stay away from it all, go backpacking or bicycling through the scenic, rolling countryside. For water sports, there're sandy beaches and inland lakes. There're plenty of campgrounds, too (see Door Peninsula map). You will need campsite reservations in advance. Sport fishing is tops in Door County. In creeks, catch brown, rainbow and brook trout, also coho and chinook salmon. It's an angler's paradise.

Every trip, even if you are camping, should include a visit and meal (preferably breakfast) at Al Johnson's in Sister Bay. Bring the camera along to catch sure-footed goats grazing on sod roofs near the parking lot. Inside, treat yourselves to Swedish meatballs and pancakes topped with boysenberry jam, an eating experience that guarantees your return for another meal.

For an even quieter retreat into the midst of this sublime beauty, take the ferry from Gills Rock to Washington Island. After returning from the island, continue to the Lake Michigan side, stopping at beautiful Newport State Park — just off route 42 — which features primi-

tive campsites and trails. The lake side offers fine beaches and privacy. As you return on route 57 to Sturgeon Bay, you'll find shopping centers with discount and warehouse stores for replenishing your camping needs. There is also an excellent camping area, Potawatomi State Park, outside the city that features a special area for bicycle campers. Be sure to climb the lookout tower. Also, check out the orchards for seasonal cherry or apple pickin'. And visit cave point on Lake Michigan, where you can walk along 30-foot-high bluffs and watch the waves crash into huge caves below.

We've never run out of things to do in Door and always look forward to returning to its quiet and serene natural beauty.

Our Favorite Meal

The Door County Fish Boil

A good place to watch it done is the Viking restaurant in Ellison Bay. Several other restaurants also feature fish boils between May and October. We've done it many times ourselves.

First of all, you need special equipment to do it safely and traditionally like the early Scandinavian settlers of Door County. A large cauldron or kettle with a strainer basket and a six-foot pole (for setting in and taking out the steaming basket).

The procedure is simple: Build a blazing wood fire, suspend the cauldron over it, filled with salted water. Fill the basket with large chunks of whitefish. We also like coho salmon, lake and brown trout steaks cooked in this unique style. Add potatoes first and later the small onions. Here's the trick — when the contents are in the boiling water and almost done, toss volatile fuel on the fire. (It might be safer to use an LP fire and just turn it up as we do). This causes the liquid to boil over with oils and residue.

You'll enjoy a whole new taste in your scrumptuous meal of boiled fish, potatoes, onions and cider apple sauce (see our recipe on page 30) served with plenty of melted butter. Be sure to have cherry pie as your dessert, it's traditional in Door County.

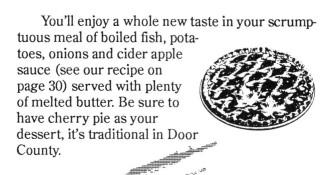

92

PART XV

Some Last-Minute Suggestions

To make surviving family camp outs easier, check into a...

Power Caddy

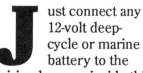

Three jacks for hook-up

Just connect any 12-volt deep-cycle or marine battery to the wiring harness inside this power source. Then plug the accessory jacks to hook up hot plates, lanterns, heaters, toasters, deep fryers, TVs, radios and power tools. A 30-amp fuse protects against voltage damage. These caddies can be purchased for under $75.

Portable Burner

This compact stove burns on butane canisters. The right weight (under six pounds) and size for backpacking. Quick setup makes this ideal

on the road for lunches. It's heat output is impressive for such a "little guy." Lists for under $60.

Bake Oven Attachment

All you need is an electric hot plate to bake on the inside rack. These camp oven attachments are about a foot square. Here's a good way to serve outdoor pizzas and pies! Lists for under $40.

Baking tray

Nonstick Griddle

Choose one with a large area for oil-free cooking. No cleanups after a big breakfast of pancakes, sausage and bacon. Look for one made of thick cast aluminum for distributing heat evenly. Lists for around $25.

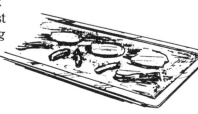

Propane Tank Gauge

Installs instantly on any standard tank for accurate readings in all types of weather. A good idea for staying alert to valve or line leaks. Shows adequate, low and refill on the indicator. Lists for under $30.

Space Saver Grill

Folds up for travel and sets up to full-sized grill and griddle. Aluminum construction – can be used with charcoal or sterno cans. Three settings for heat levels. Griddle pans double as side shelves. Lists for under $30.

Map Magnifier Light

Provides illumination while magnifying detailed maps in your RV or when on the trails. Plugs into 12-volt cigarette lighter sockets for charging. Only three-inches long. Lists for under $15.

Inside-Tent Lamp

Hang or place anywhere. Perfect for brightening up the campsite outside or safely reading inside. Good lamp for a serious card game. Runs on one 6-volt lantern battery. Lists for under $10.

Backpacker Binoculars

Features built-in compass for direction-finding on the trails. Fingertip adjustment for 3 x 28 power. Pocket-sized 2³/₄ by 4 by 1¹/₂ inches with folding design. Fits into traveling case for easy storage. Lists for under $20.

Vacuum Bottle (Two Quarts)

Keeps beverages and soups hot all day long. Features spillguard rubber seal. Vacuum insulated with unbreakable stainless steel construction for backwoods performance. Carries a family warm-up from a 10-ounce plastic-lined stainless steel cup. Lists for around $45.

Safety Vest

Added safety when stopped on the road. High visibility is provided from reflective front and rear stripes. A must for running and cycling, too. Elastic and self-stick closures adjust for comfort. Lists for under $16.

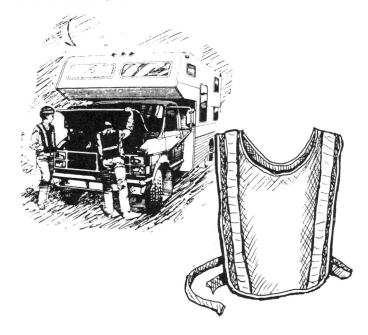

Summary

Go for it!

There's Always More

We've tried to cover the most important parts (as we see them) of family survival for camping out. As previously stated, and everyone in our family agrees, you must experience it personally. There is no substitute for hands-on experience. So go for it!

Our strong advice is always to keep in mind that you are vacationing, and relaxation and enjoyment should be part of everything you do.

We invite you to experiment and try something new. Try to photograph those moments, or at least record them in your memories.

And, of course, some of your time will be spent problem solving. Keep in mind that's where real growth begins.

Sharing is what camping is all about. You share with nature, your family, friends and your fellow campers, too. And, we hope you'll share some of your experiences with us. We'd like to include them in…

An Illustrated Handbook to Surviving Family Camp Outs — Book II

✦✦✦

Outdoor Reference

INFORMATION SERVICES

National Park Service

Headquarters:

U.S. Department of the Interior
National Park Service
Office of Public Affairs
PO Box 37127
Washington, DC 20013-7127

Regional Offices:

North Atlantic Region
15 State Street
Boston, MA 02109-3572

Mid-Atlantic Region
143 South Third Street
Philadelphia, PA 19106

National Capital Region
1100 Ohio Drive, SW
Washington, DC 20242

Southeast Region
75 Spring Street, SW
Atlanta, GA 30303

Midwest Region
1709 Jackson Street
Omaha, NE 68102

Rocky Mountain Region
PO Box 25287
Denver, CO 80225-2500

Southwest Region
PO Box 728
Santa Fe, NM 87504-0728

Alaska Region
2525 Gambell street, RM 107
Anchorage, AK 99503

Pacific Northwest Region
83 South King Street
Suite 212
Seattle, WA 98104

Western Region
450 Golden Gate Avenue
PO Box 36063
San Francisco, CA 94102

INFORMATION SERVICES

Fish and Wildlife Service

Headquarters:

Division of Refuges
Rm 670-ARLSQ
U.S. Department of the Interior
18th and C Streets, NW
Washington, DC 20240

Regional Offices:

Pacific Region
1002 NE Holladay St.
Portland, OR 97232-4181

Southwest Region
Box 1306
Albuquerque, NM 87103

North Central Region
Federal Building
Fort Snelling
Twin Cities, MN 55111

Southeast Region
75 Spring Street, SW
Atlanta, GA 30303

Northeast Region
One Gateway Center
Suite 700
Newton Corner, MA 02158

Denver Region
Box 25486
Denver, CO 80225

Alaska Region
1011 E. Tudor Road
Anchorage, AK 99503

Forest Service

Headquarters:

U.S. Department of Agriculture
14th and Independence
    Ave. S.W.
South Agriculture Bldg.
Washington, DC 20250

Regional Offices:

Northern Region
Federal Building
Missoula, MT 59807

Rocky Mountain Region
11177 West 8th Avenue
P.O. Box 25127
Lakewood, CO 80225

Southwestern Region
517 Gold Avenue, SW
Albuquerque, NM 87102

Intermountain Region
324 25th Street
Ogden, UT 84401

California Region
630 Sansome Street
San Francisco, CA 94111

Pacific Northwest Region
319 S.W. Pine Street
PO Box 3623
Portland, OR 97208

Southern Region
1720 Peachtree Road, NW
Atlanta, GA 30367

Eastern Region
310 West Wisconsin Avenue
Milwaukee, WI 53203

Alaska Region
Box 21628
Juneau, AK 99802-1628

MAPS

Superintendent of Documents
U.S. Government Printing Office
Washington, DC 20402

U.S. Geological Survey
Map Distribution Section
Federal Center
Denver, CO 80255
303-236-7477

DIRECTORIES

Campground
Woodall Publishing Co.
100 Corporate North
Bannockburn, IL 60015-1253

Travel
Readers Digest
Pleasantville, NY 10570

CATALOGS

*Mail Order Camping Gear
and Equipment*
L.L. Bean, Inc.
Freeport, ME 04033
1-800-221-4221

*Co-Op Catalog for Camping
Gear and Equipment*
Recreational Equipment, Inc.
 (REI)
1525 11th Ave.
Seattle, WA 98122

RV INFORMATION

RV ACCESSORIES
Camping World
Three Springs World
PO Box 90017
Bowling Green, KY 42102-9017

RV HANDBOOK
Trailer Life Books
PO Box 6045
Agoura, CA 91376-9885

NATIONAL RV OWNERS
CLUB
PO Drawer 17148
Pensacola, Fl 32522

THE FAMILY MOTOR COACH
ASSOCIATION CFMCA
1-800-543-3622

RV ELDER HOSTEL
80 Boylston Street, Suite 400
Boston, MA 02116

RV EMERGENCY ROAD
SERVICE DETAILS
Good Sam
Box 700
Agoura, CA 91301

RV/OUTDOOR COOKBOOKS

CEL Publications
PO Box 553
Palatine, IL 60078-0553
708/991-1270

WOODALL PUBLISHING CO.
(See directories on page 98)

GUIDES, INFO & PUBLICATIONS

DOOR COUNTY VACATION
PLANNING GUIDE
Door County Chamber of
Commerce
1015 Green Bay Rd
Sturgeon Bay, WI 54235

HIKING TRAIL GUIDE
Wilderness Press
2440 Bancroft Way
Berkely, CA 94704

FLY FISHING GUIDE
Sierra Outdoor Products
PO Box 2497V
San Francisco, CA 94126-2497

CANOEING GUIDEBOOKS &
MAPS
American Canoe Association
Box 1190
Newington, VA 22122-1190
703-550-7495

BICYCLING INFORMATION
Bike Centennial
PO Box 8306
Missoula, MT 59807

PUBLICATION FOR
DISABLED CAMPERS
Disabled Outdoor Magazine
5223 South Lorel Ave.
Chicago, IL 60638
312-284-2206

SURVIVAL TRAINING
Outward Bound
384 Field Point Rd
Greenwich, CT 06830
203-661-0797

ORGANIZATIONS & ASSOCIATIONS

ENVIRONMENTAL
ORGANIZATION
Sierra Club
National Headquarters
730 Polk St.
San Francisco, CA 94109
415-776-2211

NATIONAL CAMPERS &
HIKERS ASSOCIATION
7172 Transit Road
Buffalo, NY 14221

THE DORN IMMEDIATE FAMILY

Parents	*Sons-in-laws*
Edward G.	Edward J.
Cecilia A.	Roger G.
Children	*Grandchildren*
(In order of age)	Michael C.
Donna A.	Megan K.
Kathleen C.	Jack E.
Mary E.	
Eddie G.	*In the "Bull Pen"*
Linda J.	Tom R.
Robert F.	
Stephen A.	*Dogs*
John P.	'38'
Brian D.	'Noelle'
Jeffrey T.	
Michael J.	*Cat*
Scott P.	'Phantom'
David W.	
James T.	
Mark A.	
Danny E.	

*To correspond with the Dorn family
write c/o CEL Publications*

Index

♦ ♦ ♦

About the Author

Edward G. Dorn II, was born and raised in Detroit, Michigan. The author was really a "city boy" until joining the U.S. Army. Camping (bivouacking) was part of basic training in the Ozarks of Missouri. Later, summer camps in the woods near Brainard, Minnesota for additional training. After moving to Chicago and starting a full service advertising and graphic agency, weekend getaways and vacations were designed for the Illinois, Wisconsin and Michigan campgrounds.

These eastern and midwest wooded areas became favorite campsites to "pitch a tent" with his wife, Cecilia, and family. As the Dorn family grew (presently 16 children/young adults), so did their camping needs. These experiences have provided the background for "An Illustrated Handbook To Surviving Family Camp Outs." Many of the illustrations and photographs in this book are the work of the author who is also an award-winning artist/illustrator. Ed is currently working on another survival book about the world of advertising.

Other Illustrated Handbooks

by Edward G. Dorn II
and his wife, Cecilia

- An Illustrated RV and
  Over The Coals Cookbook
  ISBN 0-9631806-4-9

- Campers Guide to Nutrition
  Cookbook
  ISBN 0-9631806-5-7

- An Illustrated Handbook to
  Surviving Deli Counters
  ISBN 0-9631806-2-2

- An Illustrated Handbook for
  Going Fishing at the Market
  ISBN 0-9631806-3-0

CEL Publications, Palatine IL